DENNIS

REFUSE TO BE ORDINARY

10 CHAMPIONSHIP TRAITS

outskirtspress
DENVER, COLORADO

Refuse to Be Ordinary
10 Championship Traits
All Rights Reserved.
Copyright © 2012 Dennis King
v3.0

Cover Photo © 2012 Peg Fredi. All rights reserved - used with permission.

Outskirts Press, Inc.
http://www.outskirtspress.com

ISBN: 978-1-4327-9361-6

Outskirts Press and the "OP" logo are trademarks belonging to Outskirts Press, Inc.

PRINTED IN THE UNITED STATES OF AMERICA

In memory of Roy and Mary Kay

10 CHAMPIONSHIP TRAITS

1. DREAMS - Champions dream in high definition.

2. PASSION – Champions self-ignite.

3. COMPETITIVENESS – Champions crave challenges.

4. DISCIPLINE - Champions embrace repetition, habit, and sacrifice.

5. POISE – Champions relax.

6. PRIDE – Champions care.

7. HUMILITY – Champions show gratitude.

8. CONFIDENCE- Champions visualize victory.

9. CHARACTER – Champions make right choices.

10. COURAGE- Champions conquer fear.

ACKNOWLEDGMENTS

I MUST FIRST acknowledge the coaches in my life. To Bob Holden and Rege Giles who saw a spark of hustle in a pint-sized seventh grader. To Regis Laughlin who let me run the point for Gateway High. To Roger Goodling, my college coach at Shippensburg State, whose arrival on campus was a god-send. I also need to acknowledge Grace Smith, my tenth grade English teacher, who first noticed a puff of flair in my essays; and to Mr. Yarup, my eleventh grade English teacher, whose booming passion for Faulkner and Hemingway made it 'ok' for a jock to like literature.

I need to acknowledge the influence of my two brothers both as friends and role models. No one has ever had a pair of more generous siblings. To my three girls Marin, Caitlin, and Metta who are eternal sunbeams in my life. The sound of your laughter inspires me as much today as the first time you smiled up from your blankets. And to my son Connor who was kidnapped by Canadian hockey gnomes when he was seven and played center instead of guard. You embody every trait that I write about in this book. To the grad student who shared breadsticks and cheese with me, your voice sometimes edits my thoughts. And finally to Pace, Carson, Katie and all your unborn cousins, your extraordinary parents will make sure you 'refuse to be ordinary.'

I also need to acknowledge the people who proofed my manuscript when it was young and rough. Thank you to Marin Kraushaar for taking time out of your busy life of work and mothering to read my words with such care. Your insight was remarkable. Thank you to two of my students - Anjuli Young and Yoon Jae Choi, for reading the manuscript over spring break of 2012. Your comments were extremely helpful and quite precocious.

Finally, I want to thank Terri Abstein and Brie Curtis at OUTLOOK PRESS for walking me through the elaborate steps of getting a book published. It was an exciting and painless process.

FOREWORD

I HAVE HAD the privilege of knowing Dennis King for 25 years. In that time he has not only been a great friend, but someone who I admire a great deal. Our paths first crossed when I was a young assistant coach at Middle Tennessee State University in the middle 1980's. Our summer team camp attracted some of the top high school programs in the mid-south from Georgia, Kentucky, Alabama and Tennessee. The teams we brought in were as strong as any in the country. Dennis always brought his squad to camp and asked to be matched with as many powerhouses as possible. He understood that a team's summer record means nothing, but hardening his boys for winter combat was the only goal for all off-season work. Our staff always enjoyed watching his teams play because they were disciplined, intelligent and tough. Through the years our paths crossed on several occasions. What has always impressed me about Dennis is not just that he is a GREAT leader, or that he possesses integrity at the highest level, or that he is an honest man, and selfless man, but that his mission in life is to teach and share these qualities with not just his players or students but all people he comes in contact with. He has the rare ability to transfer his leadership and integrity to others. This book is a game plan of what he has done his entire life. He is a coach, teacher, and mentor to many. Throughout my life's journey in both amateur and professional basketball, I have had the sheer fortune to meet and learn from scores of impressive people. When individuals refuse to be ordinary, they often become extraordinary. I am one who is proud to say that my friendship with Dennis has made me a better person.

Tommy Smith
Director, Team Marketing
National Basketball Association

1978 Slippery Rock Rockets get ready to upset undefeated Midland High School in WPIAL SEMI-FINALS. (photo credit: Slippery Rock High School)

CONTENTS

Author's Note:
The conversations I present in quotations came from my memory and are not meant to be word for word transcriptions. I tried to be accurate, but sometimes they may only capture the essence of what was said. Other recollections may be blurred in minute details, but for the most part I think I got it right.

JUMP BALL

"CALM DOWN, COACH!"

The words were stunning. No player in my entire coaching career had ever had the bold-faced audacity to say those words, especially in the middle of a huddle during a crucial timeout. Adam stood there looking me dead in the eyes. I had just splintered a clipboard, screamed non-stop at the point guard, and was now squirming with paralyzing indecision over last second strategy. The opponent's gym was throbbing with pep band hysteria, cheerleaders were prancing past the bench, and a seventeen year-old kid recognized my bluster as nothing more than veiled panic. What possessed him to take this risk? 'I was a man. I was forty.' I was the Alpha male of the huddle who had the power to make his life miserable. I glared at him for a second or two then the buzzer sounded for the team to return to the floor. Jolted by his comment, I quickly regained my focus and barked out a critical defensive switch. An ordinary kid under similar circumstances would never have spoken up. An ordinary kid would have stared at the ground nervously shifting his weight, waiting for the storm to pass. Contrary to all predictable behavior in this highly charged public moment, Adam Fuller **"refused to be ordinary."**

My life has been profoundly affected by forty years of unintentional lessons taught to me by some extraordinary young men. In 1972 when I tumbled out of college into a high school head coaching position at the age of twenty one, I didn't realize that I had just been enrolled in a special university where teenagers were the professors. The boys didn't instruct me through lectures, power points, and smart boards. Instead, it was their actions, attitudes, habits, and lives that redefined the word "champion" for me. I slowly learned that trophies, plaques and accolades are the occasional by-products of something far deeper and ennobling. The truth is simple. To achieve excellence one must **REFUSE TO BE ORDINARY**. Only after adopting this single guiding principle can a person begin to cultivate the qualities of greatness.

As a player, I had been a diminutive, fiery point guard at Shippensburg State College in Pennsylvania. Just three months before I graduated, I sat in a losing college locker room with a face full of tears having played for the last time in front of paying customers. I was smart enough to know that my competitive future would descend into the purgatory of lunch time pick-up ball, YMCA fat men leagues, and an occasional alumni game against pimpled freshmen who didn't know, or care, that I had been the captain under their field house dome. Coaching, however, provided a seamless transition into the adult world, and a near perfect substitute for the competitive rush that all poet-warriors crave.

On the summer day that I signed my teaching contract, the athletic director told me that the team's star player worked out at the college gymnasium every day at noon. "His name's Richard Smith," he said. "Why don't you go over and introduce yourself?"

The next day I stood at the balcony railing watching a wide-shouldered high school kid drain shot after shot. I walked onto the floor, started rebounding for him, and made some casual conversation. After a few minutes I asked him if he wanted to play some one-on-one. He shrugged indifferently and said, "Yeah, aw right."

I promptly "schooled" the young hot-shot by the score of 10-2. When the game was over, I stuck out my hand and introduced myself with calculated irony.

"Oh, by the way, my name's Denny King. I'm your new coach. You might want to work on your defense between now and November because offense may win fans, but defense wins championships." Looking back, my clichéd posturing was ironic bravado, because in the most honest sense of the word, I would be the one who would constantly be "schooled" by my boys. It was through my observations, interaction, and relationships with boys on a basketball court that I slowly began to understand the ten essential traits reflected in true champions.

$$\backsim\backsim\backsim$$

That distant autumn I was still a kid when I walked into Slippery Rock High School with sideburns and a swagger eager to meet my first team. Intoxicated by the school district's leap of faith, I plunged forward with a naive sense of invincibility. In my heart, I believed that my energy and single-minded will to win would produce a Pennsylvania state championship in three years or less. I intended to forge small-town boys into Spartan automatons. We would be feared as ruthless warriors, torching every gym in our march across the hills of Western PA. Villagers and peasants would wince at the sound of our name, "The Slippery Rock Rockets."

Unfortunately, in my first year as head marauder we only won two games and both were against the same team. We beat Laurel High School in overtime and then edged them a second time on a lucky last-second shot. The dismal record of that first season was not the least bit discouraging, because in hindsight that team was stocked full of champions. I was honored and energized by the daily effort, the sweat and the hunger that the boys displayed in their quest for the golden ring of team glory.

The poet William Wordsworth once wrote that "the child is father to the man." I taught that poem thirty years ago to my tenth graders, but I never fully understood the subtle paradox until I coached young men on the basketball court. I doubt that William Wordsworth could have dribbled through a full court press, or fired a no-look pass through a shifting match-up zone, but he slam-dunked a truth that took me nearly a life time to fully understand.

For this book, I have selected the ten traits of an athletic champion revealed inadvertently to me through my four decades of coaching high school basketball. The stories are basketball specific, but the principles are universal. The traits of *dreams, passion, competitiveness, discipline, poise, pride, humility, character, confidence,*

and courage apply to all athletes and to all humans in any endeavor. Though my players were unaware of it at the time, each boy was a special mentor to me. The magical intersection of our lives enriched and emboldened me. These young men at two schools in two different parts of the country helped to shape me as a coach, teacher, father, grandfather and friend. They also molded and sharpened my understanding of the word CHAMPION.

DREAMS
Champions dream in high definition.

DREAMS POWER THE universe. Your imagination is a huge white screen where you project the movie of your future. The more vivid the picture, the more likely your dreams will materialize. The seed of a dream mysteriously takes root, but once it fastens inside the human mind, it is nearly impossible to remove.

The entire history of human progress is a tapestry of materialized dreams. The wheel, democracy, smart phones and space travel were all once wrapped in the cocoon of a dream. Dreams fuel action and when they ignite they can blaze a path to greatness.

It is critical for an athlete to imagine distant glory, to taste, to feel and to smell the idealized version of individual and team achievement. This projection into the future must be nourished with continual stimuli. It is important to feed the dream every day. A budding champion must create an internal and external environment of positive dream reinforcement. Whether surrounding oneself with dream-sharers, or soaking up knowledge from a mentor, total immersion stokes the flames of possibility.

Dreams, however, require some perspective. A famous motivational speaker popularized the phrase - "If you can dream it, you can do it." The phrase drips with inspired optimism, but unfortunately it can be misleading, and in certain cases patently false. I would submit a more practical revision -"UNLESS you dream it, you cannot do it."

Many years ago, I learned a brutal lesson about dreams during my twelfth year of teaching. I made a casual remark to my class about the odds of one of them becoming famous on a national or international scale. My naïve and insensitive statement resulted in unexpected hostility. I simply noted that in a world of six billion humans, the chances were practically non-existent that one of them would ever become famous. The entire class slowly boiled with resentment. Not only did the vocal students rise in rebellion, but the shy wall-flowers chimed their indignation: "How do you know. You have no idea. We all might do something special. What gives you the right to say something like that? You don't know! Nobody knows the future. You're just a teacher." As I lamely tried to defend my point with statistical analysis, the chorus of ridicule grew louder until I realized the absolute blunder I had made. An adult must never, EVER trample on the dreams of the young. Dreams are holy, and what I said that day was sacrilegious.

Nevertheless, it is the clarity of the dream that provides the thrust to escape the gravity that keeps us ordinary. Also, dreams are not static. They evolve through four stages: 1.Infection 2. Enhancement 3. Redirection 4. Achievement. Some people remember the exact moment their lives were changed by the *infection* of a dream. Perhaps it was a magical Olympic moment they watched on TV, or their city's World Series horn-honking celebration, or a whispered compliment from a respected teacher as she passed back tests. My moment of infection came on a Sunday morning in the winter of my ninth grade year. The Pittsburgh Press featured a story about a coach's son from Springdale, PA named Dick DeVenzio who as a 5'7" sophomore was averaging 25 points a game. The article outlined his improbable regimen of basketball development which involved pre-dawn dribbling expeditions, hours of solitary shooting practice, and a conditioning program unheard of in those days. Coincidentally, my brother's high school team which was led by a 6'11" all-American was scheduled to play at Springdale that Tuesday. I rode with the parents of a junior high teammate, and together we tried to pick out the little hot shot during layup lines. Neither of us saw anything special in any of the undersized opponents, so we leaned back waiting to enjoy another predictable blow-out. Shortly after the jump ball, my world changed forever. I was transfixed by the wizardry unfolding before me. I saw darting feints that spun defenders like tops. I saw passes shoot out of his hands like poison darts from blow guns. I saw him split defenders with two inch dribbling below everyone's reach. All night his thirty foot heaves whipped the nets around the rim. There I sat, a fourteen year old with my mouth agape. The possibilities of greatness had been unveiled. My destiny was now defined.

But a dream needs constant **enhancement.** It is one thing to declare a goal, but quite another to work and see steady progress toward that goal. There will always be plateaus and periods of discouragement and self-doubt. There will be obstacles, distractions, and naysayers who try to derail the journey. It is the dreamer who fights through the low moments, who stays strong, who rekindles his faith by battling the negativity around him who ultimately prevails. It takes "guts" to hold onto a dream.

An opposing coach in my league told me an inspiring story of dream enhancement. When he was a sophomore in high school, his father was the head coach of a major university. The NCAA regionals were being held at their arena. While my friend was shooting in an empty auxiliary gym on campus, one of the competing teams was walking through to get dressed for their 'shoot around.' A tall gangly player strode onto the floor and challenged him to a game of "HORSE." When they both had four letters, my coaching friend missed his final shot. The college boy walked backward out of the gym with his hands raised while the younger one was begging for a rematch. He said, " No, no. You had your chance, boy. Just keep practicing and maybe someday you'll be able to beat me." Later that night when the team took the floor for the SWEET SIXTEEN, my friend said to his dad, "Hey, that number 33 is the guy that beat me in "HORSE" today. His dad's head snapped sideways to look at his son and said, "That's Larry Bird."

Often, dreams need to be **redirected**. I had a conversation with a player who told me that when he was young, his only goal was to make the high school varsity. As he developed into a starter, he realized he had a chance to be all-conference in his senior year. Then he walked-on at Boston College, a Division One school and only wanted to dress and travel with the team. Later, after he got a sniff of playing time, he felt he could be a starter at the college level. Layer after layer was slapped onto the original dream to keep pace with the shifting horizon.

The converse can also be true. Sometimes a dream is too grandiose, or something unforeseen occurs. The best thing to do is adjust the dream. A thoughtful redirection can bring unexpected fulfillment. I cut a young man one year who showed up at my office the next day to ask if he could be a manager. His energy and organizational skills proved to be so invaluable over the next three years, that I wrote him the most glowing recommendation I have ever written. He eventually had most of his education paid for by a Division I basketball program that invited him to serve as a team manager for the next four years.

On the first day of school, I always ask my students to project themselves ten years into the future, and tell me exactly what they will be doing at that precise moment. It gives me some insight into who the vivid dreamers are. A rather small boy in the first row once told the class that in ten years he will be playing second base for the New York Yankees. After some muffled giggles, a voice from the back asked, "Ahh, do you have a Plan B?" He thought for a moment and said, "Yeah, Plan B is to play second base for the Pittsburgh Pirates." I haven't checked a box score lately, but I'm pretty sure this spunky, clever kid isn't playing major league baseball; however, I would bet the farm that he has redirected his confidence into another more attainable dream.

Every great champion has lived alone with his dreams long before he stood on a podium or raised a trophy. One of life's most sublime pleasures is to be surprised by a dream crystallizing in living color right in front of your eyes; however, the greatest pleasure in life (and this might sound insultingly obvious) is realizing when your dream has come true. Believe it or not, sometimes the **achievement** of a dream goes undetected or unappreciated by the dreamer himself. People can become so absorbed in the routine and lifestyle of challenge and sacrifice that they are unable to fully appreciate the accomplishment. Years might pass before sufficient reflection allows a person to enjoy the fulfillment he deserves.

Think about some of the world's most successful public dreamers: Walt Disney, Bill Gates, Oprah Winfrey, Sam Walton, Muhammad Ali, Tim McGraw, and Michael Jordan. At one time in their lives, each of them was an anonymous nobody. What separates them from the ordinary people of the world is the size of the dream that played in high definition on the movie screen of their imagination.

PERSONAL STORY OF INSPIRATION

In the summer of 1977, the world lost a beautiful boy in a tragic drowning accident. Donny Carothers would have entered his junior year at Slippery Rock High School that fall where he would have been an honor student, been a starter on the varsity basketball team, gotten his driver's license, gone to football games, attended concerts, hung out with buddies, and taken a date to his first prom. The loss of this young man profoundly affected every player, every teacher, and every resident of our little town. Though this story springs from tragedy, Donny's young dreams have affected me for the last thirty-five years.

The memory of Donny Carothers remains as clear to me today as it did in 1977. The previous school year Donny was a student in one of my tenth grade English classes. To me there is no better age to teach than sophomores. Fifteen and sixteen year olds sprout their first intellectual tendrils at this age, and they are ripe for an explosion of curiosity into some of life's greatest mysteries. In the hands of an excited teacher, good literature is the most powerful vehicle to engage budding minds, and Donny was ripe.

I loved having my players in class. I developed a much richer relationship with them in a relaxed venue away from the pressurized practice floor. Hopefully, they would see me as a thoughtful adult who cares about more important issues than their willingness to dive on a loose ball, who cares more about them defending an opinion with evidence, than defending a weak side cutter. I also enjoyed the opportunity for spontaneity and laughter that the classroom promotes. I can't imagine another job in this world that could be more fulfilling than being in a classroom full of young minds in training for their journey through life. This is true power. Politicians can claw and scramble for election, armies can invade and conquer, CEO's can manipulate market shares or gobble up helpless companies, but teachers plant the seeds that civilize the world and dictate its destiny. We launch the ships that leave the safety of home harbors to sail for distant and unknown parts.

I was only twenty four years old when Donny was in my class. I was still a work-in-progress myself. I was assigned to teach English literature so I had to find a way to make <u>Beowulf</u> and Chaucer, Milton and Swift, Pope and Keats, Tennyson and Yeats, Eliot and Orwell and, of course, Shakespeare come alive in my classroom over here in rural America. The task was daunting.

Donny made it easy for me. When the class dragged, when the students turned glassy-eyed, when they had their fill of dead Englishmen, I would ask Donny how the poem or the passage applied to basketball. He'd say, "Well, MacBeth is the kind of guy that would undercut your legs on a lay-up," or "Beowulf is the guy you want to take the last shot," or "I could feed Gulliver all night in the low post," or "I'd love to have Tennyson interview me after a game." This boy was beautiful.

What gave us an even stronger bond was his love for basketball. Once in a while a player comes along who folds the flag of his dreams around him like a blanket. He was determined to be a starter on the varsity that next year. He had been the leading scorer on the JV team, so he dedicated every day in the off-season to getting better. Whenever we had an evening workout, Donny would be sitting by the gym doors slamming a basketball between his raised knees waiting for me to get there with the key. After two hours of drill and scrimmage, he'd head home drenched in sweat dribbling up the hill in the Pennsylvania twilight until the last echo of his bouncing ball faded with his silhouette. The game called his name; his heart blindly followed.

On July 24th 1977, there was a knock at our apartment door. Coach Abraham got up to answer it. Our team manager Jay Mathews was standing there with a strange look on his face. He said, "They can't find Donny up at the lake. His clothes are still on the bank. You guys better come now." We jumped into my car and followed Jay about five miles into the country, then up a muddy road to a large pond where the local kids liked to swim. The Slippery Rock Fire Department already had divers searching for him. We skidded to a stop, jumped out and slammed our doors then ran toward the scene. At that moment a diver surfaced and said, "We found him." When they pulled his body to the shore, my knees went weak. A rescue worker walked in front of me toward the divers. I grabbed him by the arm and said, "Aren't they gonna try to revive him?"

"Too late, he's been in there for close to an hour."

"I know, but if the water is cold enough, there's still some hope. They have to try."

"Sorry," he said, pulling his arm away from my grasp, "It's TOO late."

This was my first taste of teenage tragedy. Though I would experience a number of other tragic and needless episodes of loss in my years as a teacher and coach, none would affect me like losing Donny on that July afternoon. The web of life is strung with gossamer. Even the very young must dance between the raindrops of tragedy. Nothing can truly prepare us for an untimely death – not philosophy, not poetry, not religion. We desperately seek understanding and piece together fragments of wisdom until time heals the wound.

The funeral was three days later. The little country church was packed with solemn and stunned relatives, friends, teammates, students and townsmen. At no other time is the sanctity of a church more profoundly felt than during the funeral of a boy or girl taken before their time. Squeezing into the crowded pew, every sense is heightened by the collective sadness. Every cough and sniffle reverberates in the stifling silence. The organ vibrates inside your chest cavity. The hymnal feels like a rock in your hands. The preacher seems to be the lead actor in a Greek play that we follow with unblinking attention.

After a wrenching, tear-filled ceremony, the pall bearers slid the casket into the hearse. How do you say goodbye? What do you say to a mother whose heartbreak is fathomless. How do you explain to his teammates and classmates that life is as fragile as a cloud, that all we can do now is treasure the time we spent with our friend, and remember him for the purity of his dreams.

I can't define the word "spirit." It's a word that grasps at some transcendental notion, but it's the only word-idea that approaches a description of some unverifiable existence. I've experienced "spirit" in many ways. I've coached spirited boys, I've seen school spirit at pep rallies and bon fires, I've felt a kind of spirit when Ray Charles sang "America the Beautiful," and I've known Christmas spirit and the spirit of cooperation. Through the years when I drive by a house and a young lefty is shooting in the driveway, I see Donny. When an eager hand shoots upward in class to answer a question, I see Donny. His spirit lives near or in me and embodies the hope, dreams and potential of every student I've ever taught.

I was determined to never let Donny be forgotten. We honored his memory in as many ways as we could that following season. We had a moment of silence during the first home game asking everyone to respectfully stand and remember our friend. We sewed his initials into our uniforms so that in some symbolic way he would be out there on the floor with his team. We named an annual award after him which would be presented to a player whose love for the game approached Donny's. But my own personal tribute to Donny Carothers has traveled with me through the years and finds its way into nearly every English class I have ever taught. Each year I assign the poem, "To An Athlete Dying Young" by A.E. Housman. When we finish discussing this poignant reflection on the premature death of a small town athlete, they must listen to my story about a beautiful kid from Slippery Rock, PA who used to wait for me by the gymnasium doors. I want them to know that the power of a young boy's dream can live in the ethereal world of memory. His body died thirty five years ago in another century, but his youthful dream of greatness still inspires me. Perhaps his story will strike a spark in another young dreamer sometime, somewhere.

TO AN ATHLETE DYING YOUNG (1896)
by A.E. Housman

The time you won your town the race
We <u>chaired</u> you through the market-place; **(carried triumphantly on shoulders)**
Man and boy stood cheering by,
And home we brought you shoulder high.
To-day, the road all runners come,
<u>Shoulder-high</u> we bring you home, **(in a casket)**
And set you at your threshold down,
Townsman of a <u>stiller town</u>. **(grave yard)**
Smart lad, to slip betimes away
From fields where glory does not stay
And early though the <u>laurel</u> grows **(ancient Olympic laurel-wreath worn by**
It withers quicker than the rose. **champions)**

Eyes the shady night has shut
Cannot see the record cut,
and silence sounds no worse than cheers
After earth has stopped the ears:
Now you will not swell the <u>rout</u> **(large group)**
<u>Of lads that wore their honours out</u>, **(has-beens)**
Runners whom <u>renown</u> outran **(fame)**
And the name died before the man.

So set, before its echoes fade, **(before the echoes of his running feet fade,**
The fleet foot on the sill of shade. **mourners will pause at the tomb's entrance-'sill**
And hold to the low lintel up **of shade' and hold his trophy up towards the**
the still-defended challenge-cup. **cross-beam 'lintel' of the tomb's door)**
And round that early-laurelled head
Will flock to gaze the <u>strengthless dead</u> **(inhabitants of the graveyard below)**
And find <u>unwithered on its curls</u> **(the fresh laurel wreath on his head/hair)**
The garland briefer than a girls.

My quatrain of response –

"Smart lad to slip betimes away,
From fields where glory does not stay."
But, poet, I must disagree
To live – is best, despite glory.

BEDROOM BANNERS

DREAMS

If you have built castles in the air, your work need not be lost; that is where they should be. Now put the foundations under them. *Henry David Thoreau*

Only as high as I reach can I grow,
Only as far as I seek can I go,
Only as deep as I look can I see,
Only as much as I dream can I be. *Karen Ravn*

People are never more insecure than when they become obsessed with their fears at the expense of their dreams. *Norman Cousins*

PASSION
Champions self-ignite.

WHEN NBA ALL-STAR Shawn Marion was in high school, his coach revealed a powerful anecdote about his passion for basketball. It was a cold January night after a game when Shawn was a junior. Shawn needed a ride home so the coach offered to give him a lift to his apartment in Clarksville, TN. Half way there, Shawn craned his neck out of the side window, looked up at the sky and exclaimed, "Great, it's a full moon tonight." His coach glanced over at him with a puzzled look and asked, "Why is that great, Shawn?" He replied, "Because the full moon gives me enough light to shoot all night on the playground by my house."

Two of the sweetest words that a basketball coach loves to hear are "GYM RAT." To the layman, the image might conjure rodent vermin. To the coach, it signals a player who is compelled to work constantly at the game he loves. Gym rats love the feel of the ball in their hands. Gym rats know the back entrances and unlatched windows of every indoor court in town. Gym rats can spend lonely, isolated hours shooting and retrieving without the voice of another human being. Basketball lends itself to this type of quasi-addiction because of the perfectly calibrated challenge and reward system built into the skill of making a basket. The fact that courts and hoops dot the landscape of

America also gives basketball an advantage over other sports. During the summer of 1969, a player from Duquesne University was vacationing in Paris. At that time international basketball lagged woefully behind the United States in its popularity. This gym rat was suffering from a serious case of basketball withdrawal. One day he climbed to the top of the Eiffel Tower and far off in the distance he spotted a single hoop and backboard. He flew down the steps, raced to his hotel, grabbed his ball and roamed the Left Bank searching for this basketball oasis.

The famous quote, "Find a job you love, and you won't have to work a day in your life" defines the beauty of passion. Passion is the daily enthusiasm one brings to the mission of pursuing perfection. Of course, perfection is unattainable, but the sustained quest for it is uplifting. To be passionate about something is a gift you give yourself and everyone around you. All humans are affected and inspired in the presence of passion. I spent an hour with a bug exterminator who gave me a tutorial in entomology punctuated by highlights of some of his greatest termite conquests. I was riveted by his expertise and love for his job. Whether it's a passionate teacher, coach, preacher, fan, musician, mathematician, skateboarder, poet, cheerleader or mechanic, we are drawn to the joy of their enthusiasm.

Passion for excellence inspires creativity. A young hockey player taped four large pictures of a netted goal in various positions around his bedroom to simulate the angles from which he would be shooting the puck. He believed that the subconscious visualization would give him a better understanding of angles. A basketball player painted a rim in 3-D on the ceiling directly above his pillow where each night he would skim the ball fifty times before he went to sleep perfecting a delicate touch. A football running back set up a course in the woods behind his house with imaginary tacklers posing as trees. Creatively incorporating the game into the fabric of their daily lives accelerated the mastery of fundamentals while providing the oxygen to keep the passion burning.

It is also critical to immerse yourself in the atmosphere of the contest and to be an unabashed fan no matter what sport you play. Being in the venue whether it's a ball park, stadium, arena, pool, gym, or skate park revs up the passion to full throttle. When you sit at ringside you see the sweat fly, you hear the thud of leather, and you feel your hand raised in victory.

Nobody had a greater passion for the sport he played than Earvin "Magic" Johnson. Pat Riley who coached him for eight years as a Los Angeles Laker, had this to say about him:

> **"Enthusiasm is something that comes from inside. And Earvin Johnson embodied this in a natural state. … He let everyone know how happy he was to be playing this game. Somewhere along the way he found an incredible desire to want to play basketball. … Anyone that could have that much fun on the court, even though at times he was going through tremendous pain because of the pressure of trying to produce and perform, understands exactly what greatness is all about. It's about passion. And there isn't anybody who showed that kind of passion more than Earvin." (INSIDE PRO BASKETBALL. Seabring Press. 1998.)**

PERSONAL STORY OF INSPIRATION

Give me the boy who shovels snow off the court on a January night. Give me the boy who cries after a season-ending loss. Give me the boy whose passion swallows him whole. He will inspire a coach for a lifetime.

My Dave McPherson was troll-scraggly and pocket lint poor. His hair was a wasp's nest, his nose a flattened tea-cup of cartilage; many of his teeth were blackened with decay. He was a boy who had little memory of a dad, and in the four years he played for me, I never met his mother. Circumstances that crush weaker boys made Dave a resilient survivor. He had an irrepressible will and a purity of spirit worthy of an Arthurian knight, but Dave's quest, his "Holy Grail," was simply to play the perfect game of basketball.

I didn't expect to find a Knight of the Round Table in the tiny college town of Slippery Rock, Pennsylvania, in the latter half of the twentieth century, but I'm convinced that I coached the reincarnation of Percival, one of Arthur's greatest knights. Though nobly fathered, Percival was raised as a crude farm boy devoid of courtly polish. He was a blindly loyal country waif who stumbled wide-eyed into Camelot. The veteran knights dismissed him as an eager hayseed, but Percival blossomed into one of the purest and most courageous of Arthur's champions.

Like Percival, Dave had a humble upbringing. Slippery Rock is a sleepy little map-dot whose odd name has generated some national recognition. Ever since the 1960's, Slippery Rock State College football scores have been announced at stadiums across the country as a patronizing nod to the quaint little teachers' college with the funny name. "The Rock" is now a bona fide university, but the surrounding town still consists of a handful of streets that spread out like leaf veins with names such as Elm, Maple and Normal Avenue.

According to local legend, the town's name sprang from a settler's dramatic close call with a hostile native American who slipped on a rock in the nearby creek while attempting to capture and scalp him. The people who live in the Slippery Rock area work at the college, are small entrepreneurs, or live on the tiny farms surrounding this college town. Even in this idyllic setting; however, there are still a few rural families who struggle to not only make ends meet, but to survive.

Poverty can destroy souls, or it can produce genius. To escape the dysfunction at home, Dave found refuge in the sport of basketball. Here, the world was defined and sane. He was never without a basketball in his hands, and everywhere he walked he pounded the ball on the town's sidewalks like some Puritan drummer boy assigned to a scarlet-letter sinner. The ball gave Dave an identity, and the entire town would speak of him as "that dribbling kid." On summer nights, when it was too dark to play on the outdoor court at the high school, he would slip into the college field house through a side door he had *propped open with a small stone earlier in the day. As the maintenance men were clocking out, he would hide in the locker room until the coast was clear, turn on a bank of lights and continue to shoot deep into the morning hours.*

He once told me, "It gets eerie in there sometimes. Once in a while, I imagine that I hear the echo of cheers from past college games. I'll re-enact the winning shots, only I'm the one with the ball at crunch time. I do my own radio play by play as I'm spinning and weaving full speed up the court. If I miss the shot, I just turn around and head back to the other basket to win the next game."

"What time do you usually get home?" I asked.

"Well, sometimes, Coach, I don't go home. When I get too tired to play, I go over and sleep on the gymnastics mats until morning." Dave's passion for the sport was staggering even to me, a former round-ball samurai.

There was an incident that occurred shortly after tryouts in Dave's junior year that proved to be a defining moment. Many young coaches will cover up their inadequacies by trying to appear "tough." It is a misguided abuse of power and a blurring of the words respect and fear. Young coaches often think that the players won't respect them unless the team is pushed to the brink of collapse. I was no exception. Our tryouts in those days were a three-day "test of fire." The following week the team would have double session practices with a mandatory 5:30 a.m. conditioning workout before school.

These workouts bordered on sadism. I sensed, however, that the team was wearing down. Some players were getting sick, others had blisters and nagging injuries, and it was clear that another day of torture would be counterproductive. I decided to surprise them the next morning by replacing the grueling conditioning with a chalkboard session accompanied by orange juice and doughnuts.

First, however, I wanted to have some fun with them. As they sat, sleepy and exhausted, on the first two rows of gym bleachers, Coach Will Mapes and I walked over to announce a bogus regimen for that final morning's workout. The schedule that I presented to them would be humanly impossible to complete.

"All right guys, LISTEN UP," I yelled. "I know some of you are tired and beaten up, but this morning we're gonna find out who the real men are. We're going to start off with eight 200 yard sprints on the football field--up and back. Everyone must complete them in thirty-two seconds. If one player fails to make it under that time then the whole squad will repeat the sprint. After that, we'll split into two groups. Guards will hustle over to the hill and give me twenty sprints to the top and touch the fence. While they are doing that the forwards and centers will run fifteen full bleacher steps with thirty fingertip pushups every time you get back to the bottom. After that, the guards and forwards will exchange places and you'll each do what the other group just completed. Coach Mapes, what can they look forward to after that?"

Will Mapes shouted out the rest of the torture, "Yeah, then you're mine, baby. We're going out to the field to do fifteen minutes of crab crawls, duck walks, monkey rolls, push-ups, and six inch leg lifts. We are then going to run two laps around the track carrying a teammate piggy back. Big men will pair up with big men and vice-versa. Finally, we'll come back into the gym and finish off with a few suicides (staggered full court sprints) just to work on quickness and change of direction. Damn it guys, when we get into the fourth quarter this year, nobody is going to be in better condition than us!"

The boys stared at us in disbelief. We stared back at them with cold, unflinching seriousness. After about three seconds of silence, Dave McPherson leaped off the first row bleacher seat, screamed, "LET'S GO!" He waved his arm for the team to follow, and they jogged out of the gym.

I fumbled for my whistle, but before I could get it out of my pocket and into my mouth, the team was halfway down the hallway headed toward the track. When I finally blew the whistle, the group stumbled to a jerky stop then turned around to look at me.

"Guys," I yelled, "wait a minute. I want you all to go to room 231.

We've got to take care of something else first."

As the players herded into the room for their breakfast surprise, they looked at each other with confusion, and then glanced at me, trying to read what was going on.

"Eat up, fellows," I said. "I decided to scrap the morning workout. Instead, we're going to work on nutrition."

I have never witnessed a more profound sense of relief and gratitude than I did that November morning. They stuffed doughnuts in their mouths, laughed, drank and accused McPherson of trying to kill them.

"I could see the headlines tomorrow," said Jeff Hogue, one of Dave's teammates, "MCPHERSON LEADS TEAM ON BASKETBALL DEATH MARCH - SEASON CANCELLED"

John Peterson, a preacher's son, quoted Psalm 26, "Yea, though he walks through the valley of death, McPherson fears no evil."

Steve Eakin called him "Dave McFearless."

Dave just stood in the back of the room with a half-eaten jelly-filled doughnut in both hands shaking his head and grinning. One thing became clear that day. Percival, my shining knight, would have led that team into the unholy jaws of Hell if I had asked him to.

The fire that burned in Dave McPherson was a Pittsburgh blast furnace. Steel could have been forged in his heart. He proved this to me on many occasions, but one game stands out above all others.

One night at Wilmington High School, we were locked in a see-saw game that was going down to the wire. Both teams were battling. The gloves were off. It was a Pier Six Brawl. We would surge, Wilmington would answer: a trap, a steal, a blocked shot, a full court baseball pass, a charge, a tap-in off a free throw. It was a fevered contest with both teams competing with heart and intensity. Both benches would leap up and wave towels at every lead change. The game was tied at the end of regulation. We slugged it out over three more overtimes, and were still deadlocked. Before the start of the fourth overtime, both teams were totally depleted. Sometimes when players hit the wall of exhaustion, the "fight" in them can escape like air from a balloon. Dave refused to let this happen. In the final huddle, before the last overtime, his will swept over the team like a killer fog.

He stuck his head forward, grabbed two players by their jerseys and screamed, "No one quits! You understand me? No one quits!" His teammates would never defy him. The choice between enduring private pain or Dave's wrath was a no-brainer. They bounced out to the center line with new legs. With seven seconds left to play in that fourth overtime, Dave knifed between two Wilmington players who made half-hearted attempts to strip the ball away. He double clutched and laid it in, then sprinted down the floor pumping his fist screaming "yeah" like a conquering Berserker. Two seconds later, the final buzzer sounded and the team swarmed Dave in a chaotic gang tackle. A pile of red jerseys squirmed in joy on the floor. Watching one's team celebrate a great victory on an opponent's floor is one of sport's most sublime pleasures.

Dave had an unquenchable spirit and a brave and fearless heart. I have never witnessed a greater level of passion and intensity in any player at any level. He set the standard of commitment that three decades of young men would be measured by, but very few ever attain. Having the good fortune to coach a young man like him so early in my career was truly a blessing. Through the years I have seen many young coaches who soured on public service because of the thoughtless, selfish behavior of certain players, and the petty criticism of their parents. Though I didn't realize it at the time, the experience I had with Dave McPherson launched me on a forty year coaching voyage full of confidence and wide-eyed idealism. His devotion, both to me and the game of basketball, was an unexpected gift. In any walk of life, a person is most vulnerable at the outset of their career when he or she is green and insecure. First experiences can have profound and lasting effects. They can affirm and nourish, or scar and cripple. Thankfully, a young Percival appeared early in my career to serve on my court with passion and chivalric distinction.

BEDROOM BANNERS

PASSION

Chase down your passion like it's the last bus of the night.
Terri Guillemets

Success consists of going from failure to failure without loss of enthusiasm. *Winston Churchill*

The thing always happens that you really believe in; and the belief in a thing makes it happen. *Frank Lloyd Wright*

When love and skill combine, expect a masterpiece.
Anonymous

Without passion man is a mere latent force and possibility, like the flint which awaits the shock of the iron before it can give forth its spark. Amiel, *Journal,* 17 December 1856

COMPETITIVENESS
Champions crave challenges.

Here is my list of sports' greatest competitors:

BASEBALL -Pete Rose
BASKETBALL- Dave Cowens
BOXING- Joe Frazier
FOOTBALL- Jack Lambert
GOLF- Jack Nicklaus
HOCKEY- Gordie Howe
TENNIS- John McEnroe
SWIMMING- Michael Phelps
WRESTLING- Dan Gable

Every one of these champions exceeded a level of desire never imagined possible for their sport. They all share an uncommon strain of competitiveness that has led to their greatness. A true competitor not only savors the head-on challenge against others, but he is constantly competing with himself. He can never be satisfied with any previous personal achievement. The true competitor is self-critical and demanding of himself; therefore, his coaches never have to demand anything of him. The word "gamer" describes those athletes who are productive in the heat of real competition; however, the term sometimes suggests someone whose productivity is inconsistent with their practice ethic. The thrill of competition lies not in gloating over your team's momentary superiority on the scoreboard, it lies in seeking the ideal. A true competitor approaches each game, each practice, each play, and each possession as a chance to seek ultimate personal excellence.

The term "competitor" is used very loosely in sports. I have encountered a hundred ex-jocks who think they are impressing me by saying, "Man, I'm such a competitor I even hate to lose at 'tiddly-winks." First of all, I have no idea what tiddly winks is (are). Secondly, I'm not sure that these people understand the full implication of the word "competitor." Of course everybody likes to win in any contest, but displaying ill-temper or an uncivil reaction in defeat is merely an immature manifestation of insecurity. In no way does it relate to the internal pursuit of personal excellence which is the essence of competition. Truly competitive athletes are compelled to tap into a desperate reserve of pride to overcome unimaginable barriers. This is what separates the real competitors from the phonies who throw tiddly wink tantrums when they lose.

My mother once owned a cat named Chester who was an incredible competitor. Though misnamed by my brother, my mother adored and spoiled this beautiful, snow-white female kitty. She often placed a red bow around her neck and would walk her on a leash around the outside of the house. After two years of gourmet cat food, lavish catnip toys and a designer scratching pole, Chester's worst nightmare came true. This prissy, delicate show cat had to be relocated to the barn at my brother's horse farm when my parents moved to Florida. Thrown into the murky underworld of low-life barn cats, no one expected the imperial Chester to survive a week. A horse would certainly step on her, or one of the dogs would shake her like a rag, or a tomcat would chase her off into the woods.

None of this happened. Year after year, when my parents came north to visit, a dirty, matted Chester would emerge from the barn at the sound of my mother's voice and slowly rub against her leg.

Generations of barn cats would come and go, but Chester somehow found a way to adapt and thrive for over twenty years. My sister in-law Nancy said that she had never seen anything like it. "Chester's just a survivor. She's smart, savvy, lucky, and obviously a fierce competitor."

Life itself is predicated on competition. Our survival demands that we prevail over hunger, disease and natural calamity. Thankfully, like Chester, our ancestors won those contests. The same determination and willpower that drove our ancestors to track a wounded deer for three days then drag it twelve miles through two feet of snow back to the campfires exists today in only a handful of elite athletes.

A boxing trainer told me the story of a very gifted heavyweight who was training at his gym. The boy had all the tools to be a contender. He was strong, fast, and had super reflexes. He had power in both hands and moved like a cat, but he was a reluctant warrior. As long as the opponent wasn't punching back, this boxer was brilliant. Whenever there was a heated exchange where both punchers were trading blows, he automatically clinched or backpedaled away. He didn't like the "heat" being turned up on him. Additionally, after every win, the boxer expressed a sincere regret for hurting the feelings of the guy he just defeated. He would obsess over being responsible for the public embarrassment of his opponent. In his heart, this athlete did not like to compete. Part of the allure of competition is the voluntary vulnerability that comes with entering the contest. There will always be the risk of disappointment and even humiliation, but the competitor knows he will prosper and grow stronger from the lessons learned from a loss. To the true competitor, the next best thing to playing and winning is playing and losing.

PERSONAL STORY OF INSPIRATION

Once in a while a coach is blessed with a competitive prodigy, a player whose fire is self-ignited. Stephen Klein was the poster child for game-day readiness, a walking pep talk. There are many times when a coach has to deal with teams that are emotionally flat or perceptibly unready to play. With the Klein teams, I never had to worry. His competitive hunger was ferocious and infectious. None of his teammates welcomed his pointedly blunt lashings when they weren't doing their job. He viewed a teammate's lack of hustle as religious blasphemy. His uncommon stamina placed him in a position of authority in fourth quarter huddles. When other players were gasping and spent, Stephen looked intensely composed and would challenge everyone to reach deeper.

Stephen was only one of two players in my career who I trusted enough to consult on strategy during a game. He had a precocious feel for the game as it was unfolding. If he felt we should go to a zone or pull the ball out to stall, I usually listened. It was a difficult concession of power, but he had an amazing instinct.

In the final forty two seconds of a crucial district game, we were down eight points. On two straight trips, Stephen bombed in deep three pointers. A few seconds later Grant Kennedy stole a cross court pass and Stephen sprinted past the bench yelling, "Coach, Coach, run Buffalo." I stood up and screamed the play to our point guard Sean McDougal who fired a perfect backdoor pass to Stephen as he suckered his opponent into a stupid overplay. We won in overtime.

Stephen's competitive zeal extended into the classroom as well. He ranks as one of the most intellectually combative students in history. He reveled in planting land mines in the safe conservative sanctuaries of his conformist Southern classmates. He would trample on their tenuous justifications and twist their logic into Socratic pretzels. I must admit that I enjoyed passing him the ammunition then sitting back to watch the fireworks. Almost daily, he would swivel his head from side to side refuting a volley of challenges with his stinging logic. He brought an amazing energy to that class. Some of the quieter students may have been uncomfortable with the high decibel exchanges, but I guarantee that few high school classrooms produced the consistent quality of thinking that was displayed that year.

I remember Stephen's fascination with the concept of "deism." During the "Enlightenment" many of our founding fathers were avowed deists who believed that a deity created the universe, set it into motion with natural laws, then withdrew completely to let it tick away like the complicated gears of a great watch. Deists dismissed the notion of miracles or divine intervention in the affairs of human beings. During this age of reason, deists believed that men were finally beginning to understand the mysteries of natural law and that human reason would eventually solve all social and cosmic mysteries. Stephen was hungry to explore this revolutionary concept. Growing up in the Bible Belt, he was surrounded by rampant fundamentalism at every turn which is basically inescapable in Tennessee. It seeps into the newspapers, radio shows, banquet invocations, pre-game rituals, church marquees, political races and classroom discussions. Both of Stephen's parents were "Yankees" and he helped to perpetuate the stereotype with his outspoken, aggressive liberal views. I stepped aside just to watch his combative intellect at work.

Stephen's competitive flair for a challenge was never more evident than in a choice he made for a novel he had to read outside of class. A school district policy stated that students must have a choice of at least two novels each nine weeks. Since I secretly wanted all of the students to read Steinbeck's TORTILLA FLAT, a short amusing slice of "paisano" life in California, each year I tried to manipulate the class's decision by holding up their other option, MOBY DICK, the ponderous whaling classic by Herman Melville . I would say, "You guys have a choice - a thin novelette which will make you chuckle, or this gloomy tome that will make your knees buckle." Invariably every student would choose TORTILLA FLAT. Not Stephen. He plunged into MOBY DICK undaunted. Every few days we would get an update. At times he'd laugh and say that he may have made a mistake, then a few days later he'd discuss Ahab's maniacal quest with genuine insight. Eventually he slogged through every chapter then wrote an excellent essay praising Ahab's single minded obsession for revenge.

Stephen had some Captain Ahab in him as well. A few years after I arrived at Brentwood, I started placing "Glory Blocks" in our locker room. Whenever a team won a great victory, it would be commemorated on one of the cement blocks that formed the walls of our locker room. In primitive societies a glorious victory in battle would be woven into a quilt or carved on a totem pole. Our great victories were described on styro-board then mounted over one of the cement blocks with permanent adhesive. Current players dressing underneath the glory blocks would hopefully be reminded of the glorious conquests of earlier teams. I believed that it created a link with other eras, and every year the players desperately wanted their team to be included on the wall. Stephen Klein was the only player whose name was ever mentioned on two separate "glory blocks."

His greatest high school achievement was not the night that he set the single game scoring record, nor was it the night of his first dunk. His most memorable performance came in his junior year on a night that he led his team to a 32 point comeback in the second half of a critical district away game and drilled in the winning basket at the buzzer.

On January 15th, 1992 in a game at Beech High School, the Buccaneers were pounding us unmercifully in the first half. They were virtually unstoppable shredding our man to man, nailing three pointers over our zone, and coasting in for lay-ups against our press. Conversely, their defense was smothering us. We missed nearly every shot, got no offensive rebounds, got the ball slapped out of our hands, and clanked every free throw. Beech always had deep, solid teams with skilled players and were well drilled by veteran coach Boots Scott, but very few Brentwood teams were ever manhandled like this. It verged on "child abuse." We were losing by twenty nine points at half time to a team that was our equal in size and talent.

There's not much a coach can say at half time in a situation as dire as this. The team's humiliation for once matched my own. I'm sure that I graphically referred to their manhood, but it was more important for them to visualize a comeback scenario. After five minutes of silence I said, "Look guys, we cannot play any worse, and they cannot play any better. The only thing we can control is our effort. No Brentwood team has ever rolled over and quit out on the floor. Look, we're cleaning the slate. In my mind the score is zero to zero and we're starting over. Our only goal tonight is to win this second half of basketball."

I could see Stephen nodding his head up and down. He had that squinted look of determination in his eyes. I continued, "Now, it took them a long time to build that lead to twenty nine, so we must slowly chip away at it possession by possession. If we get it under ten, hey guys, then anything can happen."

There was a knock on the locker room door telling us that we had three minutes to warm up. The boys trotted out to the floor and lobbed a few shots up before the buzzer for the second half sounded. Beech had the second half possession arrow and scored on a "put-back." We were now down by thirty one. We traded baskets for a few minutes then our press started to click. We stole the ball three consecutive times and converted two threes and a lay-up forcing them to take their first time out. When play resumed, our boys had a surge of confidence and suddenly their shooters went dry. Our press was speeding up the tempo, and both teams were playing in transition. We pounded the ball into Brian Masterson who was finally getting to the foul line. Stephen began to take over. They tried three different defenders on him, but he found ways to score on all of them. He would hit jump shots coming off of picks; he would slither along the baseline and bounce out from under the backboard to power in a lay-up; he would post up on the block then fake his man into the air, get fouled and finish the three pointer from the free throw line. At the end of the third quarter we were down by fifteen.

Between quarters I sensed an electric surge of energy. The players were gulping from their clear plastic bottles and spilling water on the mat below them. Each of them was animated, pointing out to the playing floor urgently clarifying and instructing each other in excited tones.

"Reed, come across sooner on the cross screen. My man's starting to cheat over," Brian Masterson yelled to Reed Thompson.

"Jerome, force the ball harder over the half court line so we'll get a better trap," John Will Dawson said while pointing to the hash mark.

Grant Kennedy had his palm in front of Stephen's face excitedly designing an option with his index finger, "They're hedging on the pick and roll. I'm gonna slip the screen. Look for it!"

The subs were hovering over the chairs and urging their team-mates with fiery encouragement. It was a beautiful scene of human harmony - fifteen boys surrendering their egos and wills to a solitary goal. Nowhere in the field of education could there be more fertile soil for lessons in teamwork and achievement. The horn blew and the five boys bounced out of their chairs like prizefighters. It was time to slug it out in the final round. Something special was in the air.

I had never experienced a momentum swing of this magnitude. With each possession Beech's confidence leaked air like a hissing tire. They threw the ball into the stands, missed both ends of free throws, committed stupid fouls, but occasionally sprinkled in a basket or two to hold an eleven point lead with 4:49 left in the game. When Brian Masterson got fouled inside, I had to call a time out. The boys were expending too much energy and desperately needed to rest. While they were on the bench I looked them each in the eye and said, "Brian's next two foul shots will crack that magic ten point barrier. Hey guys, we're gonna win this game."

Brian sank both free throws, and we stole the inbounds pass. Klein sliced to the hoop, got fouled and made the lay-up. They were now up by only six. The rest of the game was a frantic blur with frequent marches to both foul lines. With seventeen seconds to go it was a one point game when they missed the back end of a two shot foul. We rebounded the missed free throw and called a time out with eleven seconds.

As the boys toweled off and drank water, I talked to my assistant Tony Grimes away from the huddle. "What do you think? We're down one with eleven seconds. Should we try to score right away and have a chance to foul, or should we hold it for the last shot and just take our chances?"

Tony replied, "Let's attack. If we miss, we'll foul and maybe get one more chance."

I said, "Let's ask Stephen."

We went back to the huddle. "Stephen, what do you want to do here?"

He glanced up at the clock for a couple of seconds then said, "Let's spread the floor and go 'Four to Score'. We can get a good shot out of that."

"Sounds good to me," I said, then repeated the strategy to the team. "Ok, guys, get your hands in here." They all stacked their hands on mine. "One, two, three WIN!"

The inbounds pass was pressured, but Damon Caple got it safely to Stephen near the center line. He held the ball for three or four seconds as his defender jabbed and poked at the ball while chopping his feet in a crowding defensive crouch. With six seconds on the clock Stephen jab-stepped and crossed over heading for the top of the key. A help-side defender cut him off, so he spin-dribbled to the opposite elbow exploding into the air releasing a fifteen foot floater. The ball spun with perfect rotation, the trajectory was calculated with geometric precision. With a beautiful arching descent the ball fell softly dead center like a lunar module landing in the Sea of Tranquility. As the ball disappeared inside the net our bench erupted. A frantic Beech player inbounded the ball, but the horn sounded to end the game before they could get off a desperation heave.

As the two teams met at half-court for the ritual handshake line, I couldn't miss the devastation and disbelief in the Beech players. Our boys jogged to the locker room with their fists in the air. They already knew the significance of what they had achieved. I don't often feel the pain of another coach, but that night I could only imagine what Coach Scott felt like as he graciously shook my hand and said, "Good game. You guys made a hell of a comeback."

That victory became a seminal event in our program. The glory block was placed prominently near the locker room door so that every future player could realize the glorious possibilities that exist when a team never quits. Led by a quintessential competitor, a group of determined young men defied conventional odds by refusing to be ordinary, shocking everyone but themselves.

There's an old story about two mice that fell into a pitcher of milk. The first one swam around for a while then gave up and drowned. The second one refused to stop kicking and churning until eventually the milk turned into butter, and he was able to climb out to safety. Stephen Klein was one of those rare players who could walk on butter.

BEDROOM BANNERS

COMPETIVENESS

The harder the conflict, the more glorious the triumph.
Thomas Paine

Live daringly, boldly, fearlessly. Taste the relish to be found in competition - - in having put forth the best within you.   *Henry J. Kaiser*

It is not the critic who counts, not the man who points out how the strong man stumbled, or where the doer of deeds could have done better. The credit belongs to the man who is actually in the arena, whose face is marred by dust and sweat and blood, who strives valiantly, who errs and comes short again and again, who knows the great enthusiasms, the great devotions, and spends himself in a worthy cause, who at best knows achievement and who at the worst if he fails at least fails while daring greatly so that his place shall never be with those cold and timid souls who know neither victory nor defeat.   *Theodore Roosevelt*

DISCIPLINE
Champions embrace repetition, habit and sacrifice.

GEORGE WASHINGTON ONCE said, "Discipline is the soul of an army. It makes small numbers formidable." Historians still marvel at the biggest upset in the history of world revolutions when a ragtag band of starving colonists defeated one of the great world powers of their time. In the world of sports, one of the most inspiring upsets was captured in the movie "Hoosiers." If you have ever seen the real 1954 footage of Milan High School's improbable victory over Muncie Central, you realize that this gang of runts won the Indiana State Championship not necessarily through hustle and luck, but through discipline. Bobby Plump held the ball near half court for nearly a minute before his famous "elbow" jumper catapulted his team to immortality. The coach decided upon a daring strategy, and his disciplined team executed it perfectly.

Your future success is hidden in your daily routine. Discipline is a very simple concept. It is simply "making yourself do what you DON'T want to do." When discipline evolves into habit, an athlete becomes the master of his own destiny. Discipline is the common denominator found in nearly every successful enterprise. Losing weight, saving money, mastering a musical instrument, learning a language, increasing strength, and eating properly all involve various measures of willpower; but the mindset of a champion elevates his effort level by adopting the "habit of attack." Each day a future champion must attack his workout with a fresh vigor imposed from within. One must consciously decide to scrape away all the excuses and negativity in order to maximize the day's effort. Olympic athletes epitomize the virtue of discipline with workout routines of unfathomable rigor. Gymnasts, weight lifters, Greco-Roman wrestlers along with every other Olympic competitor, have logged thousands of grueling hours of preparation to compete for a single moment of recognition. To force one's body to exceed perceived limitations requires an attacking, aggressive approach to the repetitions. This is the *discipline of discipline* – getting one's mind and heart ready and in the highest gear to reap the maximum benefit from each day's body of work.

Everyone obviously cannot be an Olympian. The talent required to be a world class athlete exists in only a handful of genetic Powerball winners, but every athlete no matter how limited, can train with the zeal and single minded focus of an Olympic champion. Think of the enormous leaps in skill level that would result from this approach to daily improvement. Your future success is truly hidden in your daily routine.

The domino effect of discipline is also intriguing. Once a player adopts a work and "practice" ethic, other parts of his or her life tend to be transformed. The benefits of organization become clearer in matters such as time management, study habits, temper control and coachability. A stronger, healthier, happier person emerges once an athlete refuses to be ordinary.

All good coaches know the value of discipline. An opponent blessed with great talent can be neutralized by a team of disciplined players. In basketball, undisciplined players tend to leave their feet on every head fake, turn their heads on defense losing sight of their man, rarely take a charge, and often jog back on defense saving their energy for the more glorified offensive end. An overachieving team "sells out" to the little disciplines that make five separate fingers into a "balled" fist. They communicate by talking to each other in excited chatter calling out screens and alerting each other to cutters. They stay on their feet and "belly up" on inside scorers in order to maintain rebounding advantage. They sprint back in defensive transition to erase the number advantages of a fast break, and they will sacrifice their bodies to take a charge. On offense they will run their patterns with precision and crispness, patiently choose a high percentage shot, and always have at least two players in position to recover a missed shot by crashing the boards.

Watching a young player transform his life through the discipline of habit and sacrifice is truly rewarding. Players with a great work ethic often arrive with this trait already instilled by enlightened parents. Once in a while, however, inside the unlikeliest of athletes something magical just switches on and a coach gets to see a miracle occur.

PERSONAL STORY OF INSPIRATION

Someone asked Michelangelo how he created such a perfect marble masterpiece when he sculpted his statue of David. He responded, "David was already inside the marble slab. I just let him out." In many ways, this is the same process with coaches. Occasionally, a boy will come along that requires a supreme leap of faith. He has been cut from the school team at every grade level in middle school. Even though he is taller than all of his peers, they pick him last during pickup games and grimace when he drops their passes or has the ball slapped out of his weak hands. He's been labeled as an uncoordinated goober who simply stinks at basketball. It is important that a coach look long and hard at these tall, ungainly kids with big feet. They may be a beautiful masterpiece locked in a slab of marble.

Chad Grout was my "David." As a ninth grade basketball player he was pitiful - a tall, skinny mop who flopped aimlessly around the floor stumbling over teammates, foul lines, and his own feet. He played in a warped time-curve reacting to everything one second late. Passes would bounce off of his forehead as his hands were ascending, rebounds would land on the floor behind him as he started to jump, and on that rare occasion when the ball fell into his hands and he attempted a shot, invariably it was stuffed before the ball left his hands sending him sprawling to the floor in painful angles. He was a pathetic combination of Ichabod Crane and Edward Scissorhands.

At the start of his sophomore year, Chad was 6'5". When he showed up at our first conditioning session in September, I noticed some eye-rolling from our veterans. As a gauge for our conditioning program, we would time the players in a mile run at that first session. On our last conditioning day in October, we timed them again to measure their progress. Chad ran his mile in 8:46, possibly the slowest time for any candidate in my memory. During the last two laps he was listing to the left, holding his side, and wincing. This boy was in pain. As he ran by me at the end of his third lap, I asked him if he thought he should stop. He yelled out, "No, sir." Impressed by his answer, I looked at my assistant coach Wade Tomlinson and raised my eyebrows. He did the same.

During tryouts in November Chad impressed me just enough. I tell every group of players the same thing before every tryout. I'm looking for three qualities. Are you coachable? Are you teachable? Will you be able to help us win games at some point in your career? Some very talented players are simply not coachable. Their basketball values are selfish and conflict with team goals. Some coachable kids are not teachable. They are willing to hustle and listen, but they fail to grasp the intricacies of set offenses, or the rudiments of efficient fundamentals. Finally, some players have the misfortune of trying out for a team that is already stacked with too much talent at their position.

Dashing the dreams of a high school boy is the most painful aspect of a coach's job, but numbers must be limited. Keeping too many players results in unproductive practices and can lead to serious attitude problems. I dreaded the prospect of cutting a boy who desperately wanted to play for his school. After three days of a brutal blood and guts tryout in which young men leave their hearts lying on the floor, I felt obligated to give a face to face opportunity to discuss the strengths and weaknesses of the candidates I did not keep. My only rule was that they had to wait one day before they made an appointment. This allowed the raw emotions to subside a bit, and the meeting could be more productive. If a boy did not choose to have a meeting, then I would often write him a letter and mail it to his home address, expressing my admiration and gratitude for his effort during the recent tryout and encourage him to keep working on his game. I would invite him to try out again the next year because coaches have been known to make mistakes. Some of my favorite players were boys who made the team in their second or third try. I was always a sucker for those kids whose spirits couldn't be crushed, who were willing to make themselves vulnerable again. They often became superb teammates, and a few went on to become starters in their senior year.

Sometimes, however, getting "cut" can be a blessing in disguise. Though it is initially embarrassing and painful, it actually releases a boy to pursue other areas of interest or talent. High school basketball demands an enormous time commitment, and if the player has no realistic chance of ever playing, then the coach does the boy a gross disservice by letting him languish on the sideline during practice or rot on the bench during games.

A few years before Chad had his tryout, a player transferred to Brentwood from a neighboring private school. He had been dismissed that spring for an undisclosed behavior problem. Though he had a measure of talent, I couldn't foresee him getting any meaningful playing time. In addition, he displayed a strangely surly attitude. There was an air of unpredictable menace about him. On days two and three of the tryout he reluctantly went through the motions and would occasionally peer at me with a disturbing resentment. The morning after he was cut, I was getting into my car to go to school when a series of loud cracks rang out just over the hill from my driveway. I leaped into my car and ducked down. I thought someone was firing a gun, and was convinced that this boy was waiting for me to exact his special pre-Columbine revenge. After a minute or two I slowly raised my head above the steering wheel and peered through the windshield. The coast was clear, so I sped off to work. When I got to school, I was standing outside my classroom door as the students were hustling to first period. I glanced down the hall and walking quickly toward me was the boy I had cut the night before. He was staring straight at me with sinister eyes. I braced myself for a tragic confrontation when suddenly he stuck out his hand. As I cautiously shook it, he began to thank me for cutting him. He said, "Coach King that was the hardest three days of my life. I can't imagine having to go through a whole season like that. Besides, now my Dad won't be hounding me every day about basketball. I can also keep my job, and me and my girlfriend can have more time together. Hey, I hope you guys have a good year. I'm gonna come to a lot of games."

I slowly smiled and said, "Thank you," then slapped him softly on the back as he walked off. I began to chuckle to myself and hoped that none of my neighbors witnessed my pathetic drama in the driveway that morning. At least I had the rest of the day to think of some lame excuse for my weird behavior.

Though we thought about freeing Chad Grout to explore his other interests and talents, in the end his intangibles outweighed his woeful deficiency in skill. First of all, "You can't teach height!" as the coaching cliché goes. Chad had a chance to be 6'8". Secondly, he was extremely bright and a high achieving academic student. Classroom discipline often carries over to an on-court work ethic. He was coachable, teachable and hungry. We knew that he would be a monumental project, but perhaps somewhere, sometime on some magical night he would gnaw his way out of his adolescent cocoon, and take flight as a graceful and spectacular butterfly.

Developing "big men" requires a specific strategy and a willing, receptive, and determined prospect. A coach must concentrate on three areas: feet, hands and head. We must sell the player on a regimen of specific drills that will increase not only his hand-eye coordination and footwork, but also his confidence. Through a demanding

*repetition of sequential drills, a gawky young player can make remark-
able progress over the course of a season. Chad's feet were probably
worse than his hands. His running form was spastic and needed dras-
tic attention. We worked with him on "form running" with attention
to a compact arm swing, head positioning, proper lean and high knee
lifts. We also had to teach him how to pivot. He had a peculiar habit
of catching the ball then twisting his torso toward the basket to shoot
the ball rather than pivoting his feet and squaring up to the hoop. We
introduced a series of starts, stops and turns to get him to comfortably
spin on the balls of his feet.*

*His hand-eye coordination needed serious attention. In order to
develop concentration, we developed overload drills in which he had
to catch different size balls pitched at him in rapid fire. He had to
"look" the balls into his hands whether they were basketballs, tennis
balls, ping pong balls or medicine balls. In addition, we made him
face the wall with his palms up and his back to the passer. When he
heard his name called, he would "spin-hop" around to catch the ball
that was already in flight. The third set of drills included a sequence
of three simple scoring moves. Many post men have too many moves.
Great post players master only a few basic moves then use them
with lethal effect. We taught Chad the "drop step power lay-up," the
"step in windmill", and a sweet "baby hook shot." Night after night
we would pound these moves into him. Night after night we would
sprinkle water on the soil, and once in a while a tiny green shoot
would poke its head through the dirt and try to climb upward.*

*It was in the summer before his junior year when I finally glimpsed
some tangible results of his hard work. We were attending a team
camp at Middle Tennessee State University, and Chad was playing
in a JV game against a team from Kentucky. What I witnessed was a
critical moment in his career. Time after time Chad would sprint down
the court, post up strong with a low base, demand a pass by showing
his palms and jersey number to the guard, then power the ball to the
rim either getting fouled or laying it in for two points. For me, it was a
moment of sublime satisfaction to see the fruits of his hard work. Even*

more exciting, however, was reveling in the potential future glory that a blossoming big man could bring to the program. He scored twenty two points in that game. He had turned the corner.

So how do coaches inspire players to reach their full potential? Motivation is one of the least understood components of coaching. We coax, cajole, praise, ignore, challenge, demand, criticize, model, joke, scare, and bluster. The greatest motivation, however, is simply sharing the same dream with your players. The power of the imagination is staggering. When a boy knows that his coach has an unshakable faith in his potential, he will run through concrete to please him. When a coaching staff and their boys sit in a darkened gym under the main hoop eating pizza and watching "Hoosiers" the night before the biggest game of the season, and the whole team cheers together when Jimmy Chitwood (Bobby Plump) nails that elbow jumper, it's clear that everyone is sharing the dream. All great coaches have great enthusiasm, and they constantly strive to be creative and fresh and thorough. The boys know when their coaches are totally committed, when they have plunged in without a life jacket.

Coaches must be extremely sensitive to the fragile psyches of teenagers, however. It takes experience and a dose of wisdom to know which buttons to push and how often one can push them. Some players melt at the slightest criticism. They need calm, rational correction. They need an arm around their shoulder and direct eye contact. Ironically, some players crave being yelled at. They feel unloved and ignored if the coach isn't giving them some high decibel correction. Chad was somewhere in the middle of these two extremes. He could take a stinging tongue lashing, and then respond to the challenge, but there was an invisible line that could be crossed that resulted in resentment and withdrawal.

It was precisely this line that his own father crossed early in Chad's senior year. From the way Chad comported himself with adults and peers, it was clear that he was raised by two excellent parents. He was polite, well-spoken, disciplined and a very serious student, but there comes a time in nearly every teenager's life when *generational egos butt heads. In early November Chad's father asked for a conference. He was a tall, well-bred vice-president of a national corporation. I had always been impressed with his demeanor - the cool, calculating confidence of a decision maker. When he sat down in my office and began to speak, I could hear a troubled edge in his voice.*

"Ahh, Coach King, I really don't want to bother you with this, but I'm nearly at my wit's end. We're having a great deal of difficulty with Chad at home. He has always been a respectful and obedient son, and we've had absolutely no trouble with him. Have you noticed anything different in him over the past six months or so?"

I slowly shook my head, "No, he's been great for me. What kind of problems are you having?"

He cleared his throat and shifted his weight then carefully chose his words, "Well, as I said, he's always been a very good kid, but here about six months ago he began a disturbing pattern of little defiances. We've locked horns several times, but despite whatever escalation of punishments we subject him to, he continues to challenge us. It's getting very serious, and I'm at a loss."

"What would you like me to do?"

"Basically, I wonder if you could talk to him. Our relationship is not very good right now. Perhaps if another adult that he respects can approach him on the effect his behavior is having on the family, then maybe we can begin to repair some of the damage."

"Mr. Grout, I'll be glad to help in any way I can. I don't know how much good it will do, but we'll have a "man to man" and see if it helps."

It's flattering that parents recognize the temporary influence that some coaches have over their children, but it continually amazes me how much credit and status a coach gets in our society. High school sports are merely extracurricular activities designed to channel excess teenage energy. Most games are forgettable exercises in human chess, moving pieces around a board until one team wins. Yes, sports and coaches can teach life lessons, but more accurately they provide a stage for young athletes to compete and have fun.

My talk with Chad was quick and awkward. I fumbled around trying to point out the concerns that parents have, that sometimes they overreact out of love or because they are afraid of losing control. He stared at me with a look of puzzlement. He said, "Okay," elongating both syllables to indicate that he was trapped in a weird conversation.

"No, I mean that if there's friction or anything like that at home, it can affect the way you play and that affects the whole team and when the whole team is affected then I'm affected and then my family gets affected and then all of their friends get affected, and who knows where it will stop. It's like a ripple in the ocean and who knows, eventually it might start a nuclear war or something." He just stood there blinking his eyes at me. I said, "So why don't you just chill and cut your Dad some slack before you blow us all up." We stood there for a few more seconds with stupid looks on our faces. Finally, I just said, "Go get ready for practice."

Chad was unique in many ways. He was a mature and disciplined thinker. I was not surprised that his independent streak bucked the status quo and tranquility at home. He did not have any kindred spirits on the team either. His best friends were on the debate team where he excelled in the Lincoln-Douglas Debate category. In fact, he started dragging his debate partner to summer basketball practices when he was going into his junior year. Jason Jones was a slightly smaller version of Chad though stockier and more coordinated. He did have a special offensive knack that intrigued me, but my initial jock prejudice against egg-heads and other members of the nerd nation interfered with my evaluation. I have long observed that international university students have a peculiar fondness for basketball. Unlike other American sports, there is a cerebral appeal to the geometry of basketball, and a more instant sense of reward. On every college campus I have ever been to, I have always seen a handful of future engineers and microbiologists playing a random version of American pick-up ball on a side hoop. When one of their two-handed flings accidentally banks in, they jump up and high-five each other, then straighten their black glasses.

Perhaps watching one of these games gave birth to one of my secret fantasies. I imagine myself playing in a surreal pick-up game on a side hoop in a rec gym on The University of Chicago campus. I am guarding the great cello virtuoso, Yo Yo Ma. We both scramble for a loose ball, and as it goes out of bounds he points at me and says, "Off you, dude."

"No way!" I scream.

"Way" he shoots back.

I get up in his face and go all '70's ghetto on him, "Yo Momma. Yo Yo Ma."

He shoves the ball in my chest, so I put him in a hammer lock and threaten to break his bow arm. His teammate Robert Oppenheimer runs over to help. I tell him, "Man, why don't you just chill, before you blow us all up!" The details start getting fuzzy from that point.

Anyway, as a goodwill gesture to Chad, I kept Jason Jones on the team the following year despite my bias. When I was a young coach, I was jealous and disdainful of any activity that distracted my players from complete devotion to the sport. I preached a brand of blind religious zeal that breeds a dangerous imbalance of priorities. I resented any impingement on a player's practice time. My mantra to the team was "when you are not practicing, someone else is." As I aged, my views mellowed. I still wanted my players to serve a single master, but I acknowledged the intrinsic value of choir, band, church trips, horse shows, scouting, family vacations, summer baseball, concerts, and even the debate team. All of these experiences help to enrich and shape the boy into a full human being. At some point, life takes the air out of the basketball and it won't bounce anymore. A person's growth is dependent on the range and quality of his or her experiences.

Chad developed slowly but steadily throughout high school. In his junior year he got some back-up time in most varsity games, but he was primarily a JV player. He was gaining confidence, as his coordination was catching up to his 6'7" frame. Finally, as a senior he became a starter and continued to improve, showing occasional flashes of accomplishment on both ends of the floor. A year earlier, Brentwood High had won the league. This year, however, Franklin was undefeated in league play, and they were considered a mid-state powerhouse. The Rebels had already beaten us by fifteen points on their floor behind the scoring of Jason Moore, a University of Tennessee signee, and Terrell Jackson, a cat-quick slashing guard. We were having a relatively mediocre year, and the prospects for an upset that February night were quite dim.

When a team has nothing to lose late in the season, they can be dangerously relaxed. Franklin was 13 and 0 in the league and were due for an off night. From the opening jump ball, we were clicking on all cylinders. Chad was establishing himself as a legitimate force in the paint. He was completing the vision I had for him three years earlier. Time and again, he would gather in a pass, check his shoulder then power dribble toward the baseline and bank in a soft lay-up. On the defensive boards he would snap rebounds with his right hand then thunderclap the ball into his left hand before he landed. Then in one sweeping motion, he would pivot and kick the outlet to our guards streaking down the floor. Damon Caple was guarding Jason Moore. Nobody loved a defensive challenge more than Damon. He was clinging to him like a latex surgeon's glove. On the rare occasion that Moore slipped into the lane, Chad would alter his shot with a well-timed leaping stretch. In addition, Chad was getting to the foul line and quietly putting their big men on the bench with foul trouble. The game was turning into a rout. We had a 17 point lead at half-time.

Of course, all good teams have character and do not surrender easily. Franklin was going to make a run. My challenge to the team at half-time was this. "Who is going to make the big time, gut-check plays down the stretch, to hold off their comeback?"

The question was answered with 1:43 left in the fourth quarter. Franklin had cut the lead to four on a long three pointer by Moore, *then they immediately called a timeout. Their supporters were in an uproar as Franklin's five players strode over to the bench with a cocky swagger motioning to their fans to stand up and support them.*

The noise was deafening during the time out. As our five exhausted players sat on the bench with the rest of the team cupped around me, I knelt down on one knee, smiled and said, "Guys, we're going to win this game. Now, they might try something cute coming out of the timeout, so be ready to run "press-breaker." But I'm calling Damon's number this trip down. Let's run 'High-Low Baseline'. Bernie you skip it to Damon. Toome, make sure that you time your down screen. Damon, I want you to bang it in, baby!"

"Yes, sir." he said.

Just as I suspected, Franklin came out in a full court press. We inbounded to the wing, punched the ball to the middle and then swung it opposite easily handling their pressure. Franklin recovered and went straight man-to -man. I screamed out the play one more time. Chris Morman passed crisply to Bernie Cordell. Bernie waited for his screen then blasted baseline. Damon was stationed on the opposite block and his defender took a step to help out on Bernie's drive. Damon slid out to the opposite wing as Toome positioned himself to set a perfect down screen. Bernie floated a pass to a wide open Damon Caple. He had a perfect look at the basket, launched it directly on target with his patented line drive trajectory. Our whole bench stood ready to erupt, but the ball rattled inside the rim then popped out toward the opposite corner. I could hear the collective deflation of the home crowd reacting to the miss. Then seemingly from out of nowhere, Chad Grout bolted upward toward the missed shot, snagged it between two Franklin players, landed, planted, then blasted back up from behind the back board to power in a lay-up getting fouled in the process. He calmly marched to the free throw line and finished the three point play that put us up seven, where it remained until the end of the game.

Chad finished with 25 points, 12 rebounds and 3 blocked shots against one of the top teams in the mid-state. Three years earlier nobody could have predicted that a night like this would be in Chad Grout's future. It was truly the "Night of the Butterfly." Emerging from his cocoon of gangly ineptitude, the target of dismissive ridicule for most of his athletic life, here in his senior year in the biggest game of the season in front of a thousand pairs of eyes, this "monarch" beauty took flight. All I could do was shake my head and enjoy the fruits of his improbable development. I realized at that moment, more than at any other time in my career, that a coach's unquenchable faith in a young boy, coupled with his commitment to a disciplined regimen will produce extraordinary results. In the purist sense, a coach should be a gardener who has an unshakable belief that deep inside every kid lies a dormant seed of greatness.

BEDROOM BANNERS

DISCIPLINE

He who conquers others is strong, he who conquers himself is mighty! *Lao Tsu*

Self-respect is the fruit of discipline... *Abraham J. Heschel*

The hard must become habit. The habit must become easy. The easy must become beautiful. *Doug Henning*

Seek freedom and become captive of your desires. Seek discipline and find your liberty. *Frank Herbert*

Self-command is the main elegance. *Ralph Waldo Emerson*

POISE
Champions relax.

"SOME FEAR THE last shot, others live for it." I read this quote years ago and have pondered its unmistakable truth. What mysterious ingredient do certain players possess that seems to separate them from the masses? Some players are petrified to fail, and shrink from the opportunity to be a hero. Others get insulted if the coach doesn't tab them as the "go to" guy in the clutch. Clutch players have an uncanny understanding of fear and its imagined consequences. Though we often call it fearlessness, poise is a subconsciously rehearsed decision related to relaxation and breath control. A lot of athletes perform well in a group because blame can be shared, but when the game is on the line, and a free throw HAS to be made, only a handful of players relish the heat and glare of the spotlight.

I attended a national coaches' clinic in Cincinnati several years ago that was held at a big downtown hotel. I was waiting to check in behind a man who was screaming at the young man working behind the counter. Apparently, there was a problem with his reservation and he was berating the employee in a loud verbal attack. He tried to make it personal and spewed some nasty adjectives at the clerk and had some very choice words to say about the entire chain. The employee continued to be courteous even though he had nothing to do with the computer error. After about five minutes of this abusive harangue, the red-faced customer stormed off. I stepped up to the counter and was greeted with a smile and a very pleasant, "Good afternoon, sir. How may I help you today." I was stunned by his calm tone and composed demeanor just seconds after he had withstood a barrage of nasty insults. I said, "How can you be so calm, didn't you want to punch that jerk in the face?"

He responded, "No, I understand his frustration, and he's probably under a lot of pressure either at home or at his job. I just choose to remain professional in these situations."

Poise is being able to respond with calculation in the heat of pressure and chaos. Psychologists have interviewed survivors of great disasters such as hotel fires or sinking ships, and there seems to be a small subset of people who react with unusual clear-headed logic in these chaotic conditions. While everyone else is screaming and trampling on each other, some people calmly survey the scene, assess the situation and are able to survive by taking an unconventional escape route through a bathroom window or a backstage stairwell.

A great cinematic illustration of poise occurs in the movie "Shindler's List." A brutal German guard is demanding to know who stole the chicken which dangles from his hand as evidence. When none of the Jewish prisoners confesses, he shoots one of them who falls to the ground. After asking the question again he points his rifle at another prisoner. At this point a fourteen year old boy quickly steps out of the ranks and points at the dead man lying on the ground. "It was him," the boy said. The guard stares at the body and slowly realizes the issue is closed, and the surviving prisoners are momentarily off the hook. The boy's quick thinking and poised response saved a number of lives.

How does an athlete cultivate poise? Through the years a player must simply build on small successes. Whether it is hitting the winning shot in a two on two pick-up basketball game, being the last player standing in a game of dodge ball, or scoring the winning run in a little league baseball game, all of these experiences go into the bank to be drawn upon in moments of pressurized expectations. The more complex explanation involves the psychological makeup of each individual. At some point a poised athlete learns to discard the irrational fears of failure and reinterpret the moment as a gift of opportunity to display courage and skill.

There has never been a player who has come through in every clutch situation, but there are many who have done it enough, that a coach would be a fool not to put the ball in his or her hands at crunch time. Professional greats such as Joe Montana, Jerry West, Jack Nicklaus, Johnny Unitas, Tom Brady, Reggie Jackson, Robert Horry, Wayne Gretzky and Larry Bird are legendary because of the ratio of their successes to failures in pressure situations. The quarterback who stays poised in the pocket for an extra second slows down the game and gets a better read on what is unfolding downfield, the boxer who gets knocked down but has the presence of mind to get up on one knee, locate his corner and take advantage of the count to clear his head, the basketball player at the foul line who notices a defender hiding down court blending into the uniforms of the opposing bench and makes sure someone gets back to cover him are all demonstrating a sense of poise that separates them from ordinary players.

Sports are the greatest training ground for what Ernest Hemingway labeled "grace under pressure." Is it any wonder that on 9/11 the leaders who prevented Flight 93 from crashing into the White House or Capitol Building were steeped in athletic backgrounds? Their sense of awareness and decisive proactive measures defeated the diabolical mission of terrorists. The heroes on this flight understood the time on the clock, the nature of this last possession and executed the perfect play that saved hundreds of lives. I'm convinced that many of the boys I've had the privilege to coach over the years would have responded similarly under those dire circumstances. Though the artificial pressure of a sporting event in no way parallels the life and death struggle aboard the plane that day, I would definitely want an athlete who had a history of refusing to be ordinary sitting across the aisle from me on a hijacked airliner.

PERSONAL STORY OF INSPIRATION

I call it "rich-kid luck." It sounds elitist and snobby, but over the last thirty years I have observed a phenomenon that seems to defy the odds of chance and probability. Brentwood High's sports teams win more games in the final minutes than any other school I've ever seen. This is not a scientific study by any means, but I am no longer surprised nor elated when it happens. I expect it. I am actually puzzled when it doesn't happen. If the baseball team is down by two runs in the seventh, somebody on the other team will boot a ground ball. If the girls' soccer team needs a late minute goal, the ball will deflect off a defender's leg and angle past the goaltender. If the football team needs the ball back under a minute to play, the opposing quarterback will botch a handoff and we'll recover the ball on the fifteen yard line. My theory on why this happens is a bit of a stretch though quasi-logical. Brentwood students come from a world of affluence. Their parents are the consummate overachievers. Many of them are corporate executives, thriving entrepreneurs, doctors, lawyers and academic elites who have raised their children to expect success. These students rarely taste the setbacks, distractions, and dysfunction that color the world of so many other kids. So often in the final minutes of a contest, the victory goes to players who believe in themselves the most. Through their positive conditioning and the mindset of success that is modeled in their homes, Brentwood kids draw upon a history of family achievement. They visualize a scenario of success that more often than not, results in victory. They expect to win and therefore will create the circumstances to make it happen.

Kevin Thomson was my greatest Brentwood overachiever. He was almost too good to be true - a straight 'A' student, student body president, captain of the varsity basketball team, president of FCA (Fellowship of Christian Athletes) and the standard bearer for my theory of "rich kid luck." In his senior year alone, he won five games by himself with either a last second shot, key free throws or a coast to coast driving lay-up.

There was never a kid more focused or as driven as Kevin. His

*pursuit of excellence was precocious and astounding. His self-dis-
cipline transcended dedication. His work ethic was comparable
to legendary athletes like Dan Gable, Rocky Marciano and Lance
Armstrong. Though Kevin didn't have a scintilla of their athletic talent,
he manufactured an indelible high school basketball career through
determination and "rich-kid luck."*

*I wasn't even sure that Kevin would make the varsity. As a ninth
grader he was a scrawny little mouse who hadn't reached puberty.
His uniform hung on his frame like a potato sack, and his slow oversized feet often got tangled. He was a vocal team leader, finished first
in every suicide, jumped to the front of every drill line and dove on the
floor for loose balls. He had already mastered every fundamental skill
of the game. His little push-shot was released with a perfect follow
through. He religiously passed with the outside hand. He jumped-
stopped on every lay-up. He protected his dribble with a forearm
shield, but I honestly couldn't envision him running the show at the
varsity level.*

*Even before his freshman season was officially over, Kevin began
to show up behind the varsity bench on game nights. He voluntarily
assumed manager duties by giving water to the older players at time
outs, handing out towels to players coming off the floor, gathering up
warm-up uniforms and collecting the balls at half time. Eventually, he
joined us on the team bus for away games, and immersed himself in
learning the varsity system. He would stand wide-eyed in the back of
the locker room at half time listening to my strategic adjustments as
well as hearing the blistering tirades that I'd embellish even more because I had a new audience member. In those final few weeks of the
season that young man endeared himself to me by his audacious at-
tachment to the varsity. Any young player in the program who wanted
to soak up the basketball atmosphere at the next level had an open
invitation to our locker room.*

*As a sophomore, Kevin had a relatively unimpressive tryout for
the varsity. He was still physically immature and was getting banged
around by the older, stronger guys. I had to make a very difficult*

decision. In addition to the squad being top-heavy at the guard position, I had to weigh his realistic chances of ever helping the varsity in the next three years. At the time he was a frail 5'4" and 115 pounds - a pipe cleaner in sneakers with a shock of flopping brown hair. My assistant and Kevin's freshman coach Tony Grimes campaigned very hard to keep him based solely on the kid's likeability and character.

As I was contemplating Kevin Thompson's basketball fate, I remembered a clinic I attended in Chicago in the late 70's. One of the speakers was a renowned high school coach from Indiana who explained the blueprint for his school's basketball dynasty.

"The reason we win year after year is because of a simple formula. I keep twelve players every year - five sophomores, four juniors, and three seniors. I do not stray from these numbers. I am assured of having at least two starters returning every single season. These returning starters are battle-tested, experienced and form a core of success that transfers to the following year."

He then told an intriguing story, "A few years ago I was faced with a very difficult decision. When I first moved to town, we bought a house next to a young family who quickly became our close friends. They had a little boy about six years old named Tommy who played with our kids. It was one of those deals where the kids didn't have to knock to go into each other's houses or ask permission to get something out of the refrigerator. Through the years Tommy became like another son to me. Our families even took vacations together. When Tommy was about eight, I helped them put up a basketball hoop in their driveway. He would shoot on that hoop every hour of the day and night. Sometimes, I'd yell out the window for him to go in his house. I'd say, 'Tommy, give it a rest. We need to get some sleep.' He'd yell back in his little boy's voice, 'I can't go in till I hit ten foul shots in a row.' He really, really loved the game, and he developed into a pretty good player. Well, as a sophomore he was one of the five best players in his class. As a junior he was one of the four best players. But as a senior it was clear. There were three players better than Tommy. Now, you've got to understand, Tommy lived and breathed basketball. This *was his whole identity. He had put in thousands of hours of work to develop his skills and to see his dream come true. He wore the team's uniform for two years and had played in a lot of games. I was faced with the toughest decision of my life. If I cut this boy, it would absolutely shatter his life. Do I make an exception for this one young man who I had watched grow up outside my bedroom window with a basketball in his hands day and night - a boy who was like my own son?"*

"I struggled over the decision for a very long time, but in the end there was only one course to take. I had to cut him. The formula was in place. There were other seniors through the years that I had to cut who did not grow up next door to me. It would not be fair to any of them if I made an exception for Tommy. I had to stay consistent even if it meant ruining Tommy's senior year and deeply disappointing my next door neighbors."

For years I pondered the wisdom of that policy both admiring and detesting it. When I was faced with the decision of cutting a young man like Kevin Thompson who loved the game as much as Tommy, I concluded very profoundly that dynasties are vastly over-rated. The true legacy of a coach does not rest in the footnotes of some dusty record book; it rests in the hearts and memories of the boys he coaches. Kevin Thompson's love for the game earned him a chance to chase his dreams.

I kept Kevin on the team that year, then something happened which had a major impact on his basketball future and mine. I wish I could somehow take credit for the most important factor in Kevin's eventual emergence as a future starting guard. It wasn't my mentoring or guidance, nor the sequencing of drills and motivational talks, nor the competitive practice atmosphere. It wasn't the locker room quotes, the full length pictures of Magic and Bird on the walls, or even Kevin's personal belief that he'd one day lead the team. The reason he emerged as a legitimate contender for a starting guard position was the fortuitous biological timing of internal hormonal secretion - - he began to grow. By the time he was a junior, he was close to 5'9". By the time he was a senior, he was nearly six feet. His foundation of perfect fundamentals was now complemented with some legitimate high school size and strength. Though he was never overly athletic, he compensated for this shortcoming through a serious regimen of weight training and conditioning. In addition, he established a rigorous individual basketball workout which included full court conditioning drills, multiple ball-handling drills, and thousands of charted shots.

Kevin became a starter in his junior year. We did not have a particularly good season. The starting center from the previous year's league championship team decided to concentrate on football. Despite all of Kevin's off season dedication, he was still learning his position. I became impatient with him and unfairly berated him during time outs, half-times and in practice. During one timeout after Kevin had thrown the ball away on two consecutive possessions I gave him a wake-up slap on the thigh as he was sitting on the bench drinking from his water bottle. "You're killing us!" I screamed. "Take care of the ball! Keep your head up so you can see the trap coming. Fake a damn pass once in a while. You're playing like a scared little girl."

When the game resumed, Kevin dribbled past the bench and I saw some of the players pointing at his leg and muffling their laughter. There on Kevin's thigh was a faint imprint of my hand where I had cuffed him. To my embarrassment, it stayed there the remainder of the game. There was a time when it was acceptable for coaches to be somewhat physical with their players - grab them by the jersey, help them get to the scorer's table with a shove, throw a ball at them in practice. In a later era, with a different kid, I would have been in big trouble for putting a mark on a player's leg. But Kevin acknowledged it for what it was – an 'attention getter.' It was like a mother bear disciplining her cub. In fact, he chuckled about it with his teammates after the game.

Intellectually, I knew that there was no substitute for experience and that it often takes a couple of seasons before a player masters a position. Emotionally, I resented losing games and needed a scapegoat. Kevin was the perfect whipping boy. I once said to him, "For a guy who practices as much as you do, you should be a better player.

Maybe you need to shoot an extra hundred shots a day, then maybe you'll hit one when we need it." What I failed to keep in mind that year was that players are forged in the heat of game competition. During practice there is no way to simulate the speed and pressure of every variation that will occur in real games. It takes a lot of public failures in front of live fans before a player develops the judgment and sangfroid to play flawless basketball.

When I chewed Kevin out, he would look me in the eyes and listen intently, then try to implement my every suggestion. He never showed any disrespect by pouting, talking back or by using negative body language. In addition, by yelling at a kid as perfect as Kevin, all of the other players knew they were fair game.

Going into his senior year, few players ever dedicated themselves so completely to personal improvement as Kevin did. He made himself stronger in the weight room, he conditioned in the hot Tennessee sun running sprints on the high school track, he increased the repetitions of his ball handling and shooting regimen, and he religiously used a new training apparatus called the "strength shoe." This modified sneaker is designed with a flat, square wedge of hard rubber that projects a few inches from the front half of the sole of the shoe. The workouts with this shoe put incredible pressure on the thighs and calves and is supposed to dramatically increase a player's vertical jump. I believe, however, that Kevin's single minded quest to improve his jumping actually backfired and nearly ruined his senior season.

In early-January he started to have some serious pain in his right foot. He had been having a fairy tale senior year. His late game heroics defied the odds, and all I could do was sit back and shake my head in amazement at this determined kid who willed his team to victory after victory.

The previous summer I had the luxury of moving Kevin to a scoring position because of the emergence of Chris Morman, a very talented junior point guard. In a game at Smyrna High that December, the Bulldogs' Larry Daniels hit a floating one hander with five seconds left in the game to give them a one point lead. Many coaches would call a time out as soon as the shot went through, but our kids are instructed to fire the ball in and push it up the floor because the other team is in celebration mode and usually somewhat disorganized.

Chris Wyatt did exactly as he was trained. He scooped the ball out of the net, sent a crisp pass to Kevin who blasted down the court past lunging and reaching Bulldogs. With a full head of steam and one foot inside the paint, he leaped past a final defender extending his arm to release a delicate finger roll that kissed high off the glass then vanished through the net as the final buzzer went off.

Later that year we were in a dogfight at Hillwood High School against a team that boasted a 6'10", 260 pound high school all-American named Charles Hathaway. A University of Tennessee signee, Charles was truly a man-child in high school. Crushing dunks and tenth row bleacher swats were his calling cards. With eleven seconds to go Hillwood missed the second shot of a two shot foul that would have put them up by three points. We called a time out and set up two plays for Kevin, one against a man to man, and one against a zone. Both were designed for a three point shot. On the road we play for the win. At home we play for overtime. Hillwood elected to stay in their 2-3 zone, so with six seconds we ran a slick little play called "Hide." Kevin passed to the forward who had popped out to the corner. He then ducked down to the block where he "hides" for a second as the ball was reversed back to the point guard. Kevin slipped back out to the corner while the forward dragged his man back in. He was wide open when he received the pass. Hathaway saw what was developing and came flying out from under the net. As Kevin released his shot, Hathaway soared into the air like he was wearing a jet-pack. Sometimes when a player is too wide open, he thinks too much and it screws up his mechanics, but Kevin used the leaping Hathaway like a gun-sight and lofted the ball with perfect bull's eye precision just over Charles's outstretched fingertips. Hathaway's momentum carried him out of bounds, but he turned around just in time to see the net whip around the rim from Kevin's winning shot. Charles stood in disbelief for a few seconds

*then bowed his head and trudged past our empty bench toward the
locker room.*

*Kevin displayed his nerves of steel a third time in a memorable
win over our rival Franklin High School. In our own gym in front of a
capacity crowd, Franklin was drilling us. I had never seen a Franklin
team so pumped. They scored on our press every trip down, and I
stubbornly stayed in it way too long. They deflected every entry pass
and forced us out of our set patterns with random double teams. We
were losing 22-4 at the end of the first quarter and the night was ripe
for humiliation. I had already called two time outs to try to make
appropriate adjustments, but we were simply being eaten alive by
a hungrier team. On the bench between quarters, Kevin looked at
his teammates and said, "Guys, we're down eighteen. Let's just chip
away. Let's get it under ten by half time and let the second half take
care of itself." After he was finished the team looked up at me from the
bench. I smiled, shrugged my shoulders and said, "Yeah, what Kevin
said."*

*The second quarter unfolded even better than Kevin had imag-
ined. At half time we went into the locker room only down by two
points. The second half was hotly contested, but we could not get
over the hump. With 1:13 to go, Toome Brandon hit a huge three
pointer from the corner to tie the game. Both teams turned the ball
over on successive possessions and with sixteen seconds to go, we
called time out with the ball at half court. Once again it was K.T.
time. We decided to hold the ball for the last shot. We would use our
four corner delay until there were ten seconds left, and then run our
"Open" play for Kevin. He would get a high pick then make a decision to drive, shoot or dish. Franklin decided not to pressure Kevin
out by the mid-court line. He tucked the ball under his chin in triple
threat then waited. When the defender edged closer, he would jab-
step to keep him honest. With five seconds left Kevin knifed down
the key between collapsing defenders. He jumped in the air to shoot
a leaning twelve footer when Franklin's Tory Lane swatted the shot
away barely swiping Kevin's shooting arm in the process. An astute*

and courageous referee blew his whistle and with two seconds left Kevin Thompson was shooting two shots to win the game. Franklin called a timeout to ice the shooter, but when the horn sounded, he marched to the line and popped in his first shot dead-center to take our only lead of the night. On the second shot he purposely misfired so that time would elapse. The ball bounced to the corner and they called their final time out with 8 tenths of a second left in the game. On the inbounds play, Tory Lane caught a long pass on the opposite sideline, heaved a fade away hook shot that hit the guide wires above the backboard. Our students swarmed the floor, hoisted Kevin on their shoulders and carried him out of the gym like a conquering Roman general.

A few days later the doctors determined that Kevin had been playing with a severe stress fracture in a metatarsal bone in his right foot. It was on the verge of becoming a full blown break. He would be out for six weeks. We might get him back for the last game of the regular season, but I was sure that he would never again play like the warrior he had been earlier in his senior season. To this day I blame the "strength shoes" that he trained with all summer. The unnatural skeletal stress that those shoes place on a young man's feet and legs can be debilitating. Perhaps in Kevin's zeal, he simply pushed himself beyond what normal players are capable of. In any event, our leading scorer, team captain and player-coach would be sidelined for a very long time.

By the time that Kevin returned in late February, we had plugged the hole as best we could and had found a different chemistry. We had one game left at Mt. Juliet, and we needed a win on their floor to secure the regular season district title. Kevin began to practice during that last week, and although he was still clearly hobbled, the doctor cleared him to play. We beat Mt. Juliet easily, then won our first two tournament games before facing Beech High School in the championship game. Kevin played sparingly in those games, and even though he was not a hundred per cent, I decided to start him against Beech. We got pounded by sixteen, but by losing, we serendipitously stayed out of the tougher bracket in the regional tournament the following week. Nobody wanted any part of Clarksville High School who was the pow- erhouse of the mid-state. In addition to a 6'10" center and some rugged street savvy guards, Clarksville had two future NBA players on their roster - 6'5" Trenton Hassel who was drafted in the second round by the Chicago Bulls after a stellar career at Austin Peay State University, and 6'7" Shawn Marion, a first round draft choice of the Phoenix Suns, a future NBA all-star, a member of the 2004 Olympic Dream Team and a starter on the 2011 World Champion Dallas Mavericks.

In the regional tourney we won two exciting games- one against Northeast High School, and the other against Smyrna High school in a rubber match. Kevin was getting stronger each game, and was be- ginning to play with the confidence of a few months earlier.

Clarksville destroyed both of their opponents, one of which was our league's tournament champion Beech High School who they beat by seventeen points. This set up a showdown between Brentwood High School and Clarksville High school for the Region 6 AAA championship.

What happened that night is still a mystery to me. Call it divine intervention, call it a snag in the cosmic fabric of the universe, call it rich-kid luck, call it anything you want, but I call it one of the most perfect games ever played by a high school team. The regionals were played over a three day period. There was no break. After our semi- final win, I mapped out the championship game plan in the locker room before the boys got on the bus. I said, "Listen up! Here's the way we're gonna win tomorrow night. I want you to rehearse it tonight in your dreams. Number one: Offensively, we will start off the game in our "four to score" offense to spread them out and get their big guys away from the basket. We'll mix in a little "Clarion" (our continuity delay game) and we'll occasionally 'pot-shot' them with a back door cut. WE WILL CONTROL THE TEMPO. Number two: Defensively, we will run a diamond and one defense to slow down Shawn Marion. Toome, you will chase him everywhere on the court, deny him the ball as much as possible, breathe on him every time he shoots, then

block him out on every shot. The other four guys will be in a tight diamond formation and dare them to take the outside shot. They will get
ZERO second shots. All right, let's get on the bus and sweet dreams."

I could sense a buzz at school the next day. Our boys were ready
to go. There's nothing like being in the "main event." We had a brief
walk-through after school then boarded the bus around five. We arrived around half time of the consolation game and as we walked
through the packed gym to our locker room, every head turned to
size us up.

Ten minutes before we took the floor we reviewed our strategy
one more time. When the consolation game ended, we were chomp-
ing at the bit waiting to do battle. If a neutral observer watched the
two teams warm up, it would have been inconceivable to think we
could win. They had the size, grace and the confidence of a Division
I college basketball team. Strangely enough, our 6'3" center won the
jump ball and the game plan was set in motion.

It worked beautifully in the first half. Our first possession set the
tone for the whole game. We held the ball for over a minute before
Toome Brandon nailed an incredibly deep three pointer. On defense,
Marion got far fewer shots than he was accustomed to, they shot er-
ratically from the outside, and we gang rebounded every missed shot.
We went into the locker room up nine points. As their team left the
floor, they were bickering with each other while our guys dashed to
the locker room beaming and screaming.

My half time speech was brief. "Guys, we're executing perfectly.
Now, they're gonna turn up the heat and make a run. When they
clamp on their press, we attack it. If we don't have the lay-up, bring
it back out and let's do some more surgery on offense. Every possession, EVERY POSSESSION is critical. Talk to each other out there,
block out, take care of the ball. If we do that, fellows, we're gonna be
famous."

We had the possession arrow for the second half. For the opening
play, I decided to call a cute little "rub-off" screen for an alley-oop to
Josh Van Horne. Kevin floated a perfect pass toward the basket and

Josh timed it perfectly. He caught it in the air and banked it above the rim. Hassel and Marion both reacted too late and swatted at air before bumping Josh's body on the way down. Josh made the free throw and the rout was on.

With five minutes left to go in the game, we led by twenty five points. Our little hustling over-achievers were pounding a team with two future pros. It was the "perfect storm" of championship games. It was a night that coaches envision in their dreams. Twelve gifted boys were working together like the gears of a Swiss clock, perfectly in synch with the moment, energized in the pursuit of glory, in love with the game and each other, swirling around the floor in a beautiful symphony of movement, and I - I was their Toscanini waving the baton in a state of complete and utter rapture.

Kevin Thompson was the heart and soul of that team. Without his return, that glorious victory would never have happened. His poise, mental toughness, intelligence, discipline and spiritual strength inspired his team and his coaches. Sports create scenarios of artificial conflict. They are designed to entertain as well as to teach. But why do some young men respond better than others in these contrived pressure situations? Kevin seemed to thrive in those moments of great drama while most basketball players are secretly afraid to take the last shot. They simply don't want the responsibility or the label of "choker." Their fragile egos can't handle the potential focus of public failure. I'm positive that Kevin's remarkable trait of "grace under pressure" will transfer to the way he handles all crises in his life. He will simply face it head-on, trust his gut to make the right call, and not be cowed by imaginary consequences.

I watched this young man hone his unflappable personality over four years. The only credit I deserve is for the numerous opportunities I gave him to practice the Christian virtues of patience and tolerance. I was forty-one years old when I met him, yet he revealed a precocious sense of self-assurance and optimism that I have yet to achieve. Maybe someday when he's governor of Tennessee he will tell me his secrets (and maybe appoint me his secretary of education).

BEDROOM BANNERS

POISE

Poise: the ability to be ill at ease inconspicuously.
Earl Wilson

A cheerful frame of mind, reinforced by relaxation... is the medicine that puts all ghosts of fear on the run.
George Matthew Adams

Always keep your composure. You can't score from the penalty box; and to win, you have to score." *Bobby Hull*

Lone eagles soaring in the clouds,
Fly with silent, peaceful poise.
While turkeys, in their earth-bound crowds,
Fill the atmosphere with noise. *William Arthur Ward*

DREAMS: Donny Carothers - #24 back row. (photo credit: Slippery Rock High School)

PASSION: Dave McPherson elevates for two vs. Mars High School 1976. (photo credit: Slippery Rock High School)

COMPETITIVENESS: Stephen Klein glides
in for a layup vs. Beech High School, 1992.
(photo credit: Brentwood High School)

DISCIPLINE: Chad Grout 'returns to sender'- 1994. (photo credit: Brentwood High School)

POISE: Kevin Thompson drives to hoop in playoff game-
1995 sub-state. (photo credit: Brentwood High School)

PRIDE: Point guard Danny Krow posts up in the paint. (photo credit: Brentwood High School)

HUMILITY: Anvil Nelson supporting the football Bruins. Counting down the days to B-ball 2009. (photo credit: Brentwood High School)

CHARACTER: #22 sophomore Stan Sabin 1974.

CONFIDENCE: A.J. Krow weaves through the press vs.
Overton 2008. (photo credit: Brentwood High School)

COURAGE: John Boucher baby hook vs. Oakland 1987. (photo credit: Brentwood High School)

TRAIT **6**

PRIDE
Champions care.

WHEN I TAUGHT the <u>Declaration of Independence</u> to my students I would use an unconventional lesson plan. I would divide the class into colonies who were responsible for rewriting Thomas Jefferson's document into simpler language. We then imaginatively reinvented history by having the representatives from each colony sail across the Atlantic to personally read their grievances to King George III, a petty tyrant with an objectionable personality. On the day of their presentations, I would have a student wheel me in on a portable throne (a cafeteria chair precariously placed on an AV cart). I would wear a robe and a Burger King crown and act as obnoxious as I could when they read their complaints about my taxes, stamps and quartering of troops. One year in the middle of one of my royal tirades I crossed the line when I commanded my sergeant-at-arms to fetch that foul piece of red, white and blue cloth hanging above the chalk board. I would show these filthy colonists how I felt about their flag. Most of the students were laughing as I arrogantly grabbed the flag and acted like I was going to tear it in half. All of a sudden I heard a shout and a crash in the back of the room. A boy was sprinting straight up the center aisle toward my portable throne screaming, "DON'T YOU TOUCH THAT FLAG. YOU HEAR ME!" In his haste he bumped the cart, and

I dangerously tetered in my chair trying to maintain my balance. If I had toppled from that chair, he possibly could have killed the King of England that day. After I regained stability, I broke character and calmly told him to settle down. I said it was just a skit. He said, "I know, but that flag is bigger than a skit. My Uncle died in Viet Nam. Nobody disrespects the flag he fought for."

The student was absolutely right. I had made a serious misjudgment in my improvisation that day. I should have known better. Some symbols are too sacred and should never be misused. That boy's pride in the flag and everything it stands for taught me a powerful lesson.

Pride manifests itself in every human endeavor. When I take an evening walk in my neighborhood, a quick glance at the landscaping speaks volumes about the level of pride the owners have in their property. One house in particular impresses me with the meticulous care that has been given to every bush, tree, plant and blade of grass. The house is owned by an old Japanese couple who are broadcasting to the world the pride they have in the beauty of their perfectly manicured lawn.

How you dress, how you talk, how you play, and how you live will determine how you are remembered. Your signature is on everything you do, so make sure it reflects the pride that you have in yourself. A teaching colleague Ron Riddle uses the phrase, "When your name is on the side of the truck, you better stand by your work." The same is true in sports. Watch how a team warms up before a game, and you can get an excellent read on the amount of pride the coach has in his or her program. If the team straggles onto the floor, shoots lazy circus shots in the layup lines or they talk to their friends in the bleachers, they will not be ready to play hard at tip-off and the coach is totally to blame. However, you can tell which coaches have pride in the way their teams prepare to compete. If they warm up with snappy purpose, if there is a thoughtful sequence of drills incorporating fundamentals and slices of game conditions that prime a team to blast out of the starting gate, then most likely they'll have a good sweat going and be ready to rumble from the jump ball. Additionally, much can be gleaned from where the players' eyes are focused in the huddle during timeouts, and how the players on the end of the bench conduct themselves throughout the game. In a program with pride, five players are on the floor, but all twelve are in the game.

I am fascinated by cable shows about raw nature. I never understood why an extended family of lions was called a "pride;" however, after watching the teamwork and ferocity with which they hunt, defend their young and protect their territory it became more than obvious. In humans "pride" can simply be defined as the strength of belief one has in his own convictions. How strongly does one believe in his country's freedoms? How strongly does one believe that illicit temptations should be resisted? How strongly does an athlete believe that he or she deserves to win? Each of these examples is related to the level of pride inherent in the individual.

The word "pride" is multifaceted. It has several uses and some are negative. People can exhibit a wholesome pride in their school, family, appearance, friends, and talents; however, the word can have a negative connotation when it crosses over into a form of self-love that becomes destructive. When pride slides into vanity or obstinacy it usually produces negative effects. Stubborn pride ruins relationships, arrogant pride ruins reputations and diminishes achievements. The poem "Ozymandias" by Percy Bysshe Shelly captures the folly of unchecked hubris better than anything ever written. The poet describes an ancient ruler's shattered monument discovered in a desert with its head buried face down in the endless sand that was once his mighty empire. The words he had engraved on the pedestal read, "LOOK ON MY WORKS YE MIGHTY AND DESPAIR!" The irony is inescapable. This pathetic egomaniac, so desperate for immortality, was in reality nothing more than a delusional blustering tyrant.

When pride is channeled for positive goals, then greatness is attainable. Pride is a sense of connection, worthiness, and achievement. It is a tangible emotion that both reflects and shapes action. When an athlete makes himself "reach down" inside himself to find that "something extra" that he is not absolutely sure is there, he taps into a mystical world of self-understanding. One of the most inspiring examples of this was in the 2008 Summer Olympics in Beijing, China when Michael Phelps was in the process of winning an unbelievable eight gold medals in swimming. For him to achieve this remarkable feat, however, he needed the help of some relay partners. In the 4 x 100- meter freestyle relay, his team had slipped into a distant second place when the final leg began. Michael had swum the third leg and his quest for a gold medal sweep seemed derailed. With 50 meters to go, his teammate Jason Lezak began to close the gap on France's final swimmer who anchored the fastest relay team that France had ever assembled, and who many experts predicted would win the gold. With about 10 meters to go, the impossible merged into the probable. Phelps, his teammates and about 30 million Americans screamed with disbelief and encouragement as two sets of opposing fingertips lunged to touch the wall. Lezak had done it. The National Aquatic Center erupted into pandemonium. By a mere four one-hundredths of a second 3:08.28 to France's 3:08.32, the Americans won, and preserved the opportunity for Michael Phelps to continue his historic pursuit of Olympic perfection.

It is in these triumphant moments that we witness the power of pride. Reaching as deep into the well of human courage that any athlete has ever done, Jason Lezak's effort served as one of the most singular examples of "refusing to be ordinary." Pride in himself, pride in his teammates, and pride in his country spurred him to victory. Jason Lezak trained a lifetime for this one moment, and he will forever be connected to one of sports' most glorious stories.

PERSONAL STORY OF INSPIRATION

For years I thought I would never again coach a point guard who was cast from the same mold as Dave McPherson, my first tenacious scrapper from Slippery Rock. Though Danny Krow played with the same bravery and passion, the two of them could not have come from more diametrically opposite family environments. Dave's home was borderline dysfunctional and poor, Danny Krow's home was thriving, supportive and wealthy. In the age-old debate over which is the more powerful shaping influence- NATURE or NURTURE, I'm more inclined to go with NATURE. When I watched Danny Krow play to the point of absolute exhaustion night after night, diving on loose balls, and sacrificing his body to take charges, it became clear that the qualities of athletic determination and pride are genetically encoded and not necessarily the result of shaping forces. In addition, the myth that rich kids were soft, spoiled and prone to materialistic distraction was quickly debunked when I moved to Brentwood and completely negated by Danny Krow's pride in everything he attempted.

Danny was the oldest of three boys from a family of Italian descent. His dark large eyes combined with a Mediterranean complexion gave him a handsomely exotic look. Danny celebrated his Italian heritage at every turn by flaunting his ethnic links in his choice of music, clothing, and movies. Sinatra was cool, silk shirts were cool and the "The Godfather" trilogy was his favorite DVD. Back in Philadelphia where his family is from, he would have been just another kid down the block. In the cornbread South, he was Michael Corleone in Nikes, a self-confident and happy kid, brimming with enthusiasm who lived for the Tuesday and Friday night hardwood wars.

Though his fondness for things Italian added some spice to his public persona, at his core he was simply a driven winner. Unlike a few of my former players who were gifted scholars, Danny was an average student, but there were expectations from home that demanded he excel. He would agonize over a bad grade on a vocabulary quiz. When he would get a low score back, he would pound his desk with his fist. "Dang, I studied for this quiz and all I got was an 84%. I swear I knew these words."

When we went over the correct answers on a major literature test, he would stubbornly argue over an answer until I would finally have to cut him off. He was a classic first born male who was determined to be an achiever so that his parents could be proud of him. This is the kind of ego that coaches love - a boy with an irrepressible will, eager to challenge, unafraid to fail, who will bounce up off the floor faster than he got knocked down.

Between his junior and senior year he was a "beast" in the weight room. Many of his closest friends were football players, and they got him hooked on the sound of clanging metal and posing in front of mirrors. It paid big dividends on the basketball court in his rebounding, defense, and endurance; but it also put a misguided notion into his head about trying to score on the inside.

There is a phenomenon in basketball that every coach is aware of. Big men want to be guards, and guards want to be big men. Danny was no exception. Because of the strength advantage that he gained in the weight room, he was under the delusion that he could take anybody inside, no matter what size. Game after game he would bulldoze his way onto the block, call for the ball then pump fake several times before trying to power in a lay-up. At first we had some polite discussions about the ineffectiveness of this strategy, but he doggedly tried to prove me wrong. Occasionally, he would overpower a little guard and score, then smugly glance over at me as he ran down the floor. Too often, however, a legitimate big man would come over to help out and punish Danny for trespassing by swatting his shot. I finally had to impose a modified "Morman" rule on his inside shots.

The "Morman" rule was instituted about eight years earlier in honor of Chris Morman, the poorest shooting point guard in Brentwood history. Chris was a very effective player, but he didn't fully realize what a lousy shooter he was. I decided to limit the number of outside shots he was allowed to take. I didn't want to tell him that he was forbidden to shoot, because teams would completely back off of him and clog the lane, so I enforced a two shot limit. Actually, he was required to take two shots per game just to bluff the other team; for every shot that Chris made, he was rewarded with another attempt. I thought it was a fair and creative compromise, and Chris reluctantly accepted it for the good of the team. For Danny, I limited his inside pump fake fiesta to one per game. If he made it, then he would be allowed another attempt.

Danny's physical skills were limited even for a high school athlete. He did not have quick feet, his reaction time was average, and he was not a particularly good outside shooter. For some reason this dominantly left handed kid had grown up shooting with his right hand. But Danny's "intangibles" were priceless. True leaders don't demand respect, they inspire it. There is an attitude, a posture, a genuine honesty that screams "follow me" to the other players. This is the kind of kid who needs to have the ball in his hands at "crunch time." He's not afraid to fail. His self-esteem is too entrenched, too resilient.

Danny's parents deserve all the credit for his remarkable character. Though the family enjoyed the bountiful fruits of some hard-earned corporate "ladder climbing," both of them had lower middle class backgrounds. They made absolutely sure that Danny and his brothers grew up with those same values. Unlike many of the students at Brentwood who are shamelessly indulged, Danny was on a very strict budget. His frugality became legendary among the players. On road trips he would skip meals at our "fast food" stops, saving the money for an upcoming concert or for gas money. The voice mail on his cell phone had this message: "Hi, this is Danny. You all know my rate plan, so unless you have an urgent message, just call me back later, see ya." I remember seeing Patrick Micklewright shaking his head one night at a McDonalds, looking at Danny Krow and saying out loud, "He's the cheapest son of a bitch on earth."

Though Danny competed with ferocity on the basketball court, he was also a ferocious fan for his favorite sports teams. His passion was infectious whether it was for the Florida State Seminoles, the Tennessee Titans, or for his friends who played on the Brentwood High football team. In Danny's senior year, the football Bruins made a remarkable run to win the Tennessee 5-A state championship. He was one of the team's most loyal fans - a tail-gating, face-painting, towel waving, unabashed maniac. A week earlier he had to miss the historic upset of Germantown High School in Memphis, because our basketball team was in a Thanksgiving tournament in Hendersonville. On the bus trip home, Danny was on the cell phone yelling out updates to the whole bus who would erupt in cheers. I guess there were a few times when his "rate plan" didn't matter.

Danny Krow did everything full-bore. Even his high school romance was a raging soap-opera. For most of his high school career, he dated a lovely and equally competitive girl who played on the girls' basketball team. Their blow-ups, feuds, make-ups and hallway verbal skirmishes were relentless. It was the most volatile chemistry I have ever witnessed. It slowly went from the sublime to the ridiculous. Eventually, Danny's mother called me and asked me to talk to him. She felt that this teenage relationship was becoming unhealthy if not borderline psychotic. I called him into my office and broached the subject from the basketball angle. I wanted to know if all of this public wrangling was going to take his mind off of basketball. He said, "Ah, Coach, that's just how we relate. It's just a way for us to keep things interesting. Who wants to have a boring relationship? Believe me, Coach, I am one hundred percent committed to getting the job done this season."

I thought to myself, "Heck, that's all I need to know."

Another endearing quality that Danny had was a sense of compassion. He reminded me of another player from many years earlier named Rob McConnell. Rob was involved in a special moment at the end of a Christmas tournament championship game against Glencliff High School which profoundly affected me. We had been winning the entire game. With four seconds left, the other team stole a pass and scored to go up by one. Our captain, Kevin Whitehurst, immediately called a timeout. We set up our full court desperation play called "double deep." If it is executed perfectly, two guards sweep in a criss-crossing pattern under the hoop; the ball is thrown from the opposite baseline at a diagonal to a designated spot on the wing. Hopefully, one of the guards arrives for a catch and final shot.

The play unfolded perfectly. Matt Dale fired a high arching pass over their hovering half court press. One of Glencliff's players leaped to deflect it, but mistimed his jump. The ball floated precisely into Kevin's hands as he circled out to the wing. He pivoted to shoot and had an uncontested look at the rim. He released the ball with beautiful *rotation, but it bounced off the back of the rim as the horn sounded. Kevin stood motionless on the floor, bent over, and flushed with disappointment. As the Glencliff players and fans skipped around the floor in celebration, Rob McConnell left our bench, walked straight out to the floor and wrapped his arms around the crestfallen Kevin. The two of them walked silently to the locker room together with Rob's arm on Kevin's shoulder. It was a remarkable gesture of tenderness and consolation that I have never forgotten.*

Danny had a noble streak of compassion as well. So often a high school jock can deceive himself into overestimating his importance. He sees his name or picture in the paper. His family plans their lives around his games. A storeowner or businessman might recognize him up-town or at the mall. Some freshmen girls might giggle in adulation when he passes by. He might get a form letter from a college and think it's a scholarship offer, but ninety nine percent of these high school heroes will have their balloon popped soon after graduation. Danny was too grounded to let this happen.

During his junior and senior year, he took a young man under his wing in a wonderful gesture of friendship. The boy had severe learning disabilities but came to all of our games just to root for Danny. I would often see the two of them sitting together in the bleachers before ball games or laughing and interacting with each other in the hallways during school. There was a genuine enjoyment of each other's company, and Danny's example opened the door for Chris to get a taste of mainstream life in a big high school. There was nothing patronizing or phony in their relationship. Danny's heart was big enough to include some unlikely friends, and I'm sure that he would admit to benefiting from the friendship as much as Chris.

Danny led the team to a 22-9 record in his junior year. In his senior year we were 23-7. Though he had never envisioned himself as point guard, he was thrust into the role in the middle of his sophomore year. He developed a knack for advancing the ball down court better than any previous guard I had ever coached. When an opponent would score a basket, our team was trained to sprint to designated spots on the court. Danny would catch the inbounds pass and often without a dribble, launch a full court push pass into the hands of a streaking Josh Brennard or Ian Van Horne who would constantly beat the opposing big men down court. Danny's ability to see the floor and judge the long pass was uncanny.

In his junior year we made it to the District Championship game against Franklin High. We were down by ten at halftime but battled back to tie the game with eight seconds to play. We fouled their star guard Cody Waddy who missed the second of his two free throws. Danny got the outlet pass from Patrick Micklewright and heaved it up the court to Tyler Cole who swept in for what appeared to be a game winning lay-up. Franklin's best athlete, Phillip Williams, came out of nowhere to catch Tyler and leaped to get a piece of both the ball and his arm. The ball careened awkwardly off the rim and into the hands of Walker Campbell who whipped the ball to the top of the key where Danny was quickly trailing the play. The horn went off as Danny launched a shot from the top of the key that he had practiced over a million times both in the gym and in his head. As the ball traced its slow arc toward the basket, I crouched with my hands balled into fists ready to explode in a flailing leap, but the ball clanked off the back of the rim and bounced aimlessly away.

There was no Rob McConnell to comfort Danny with a hug that night. If God were a film director, he would have scripted the shot to have gone in. Danny deserved a moment like this in his full-throttled career. My only words of consolation today are that memories are imprecise things. When I attended my twentieth high school reunion, I was walking toward a number of girls (women) who were huddled in the hallway of the hotel ballroom. One of them swung around and said, "Hey, we were just talking about you!" and they all quickly converged around me. One of them said excitedly, "We were remembering the half-court shot you made to beat Penn Hills in the last basketball game of our senior year. That was so dramatic. And beating our arch-rival was just awesome."

I paused in momentary confusion then decided to smile sheepishly, shrug my shoulders and nod my head in agreement. I said, "Yeah, that was great."

The truth was, however, that I had fouled out of the game and was sitting on the bench while my brother Dave ran the point. With two seconds left in the game, Brian McMahon had launched an errant 30 footer over top of George Karl (future Denver Nuggets coach) that Ronnie Jancula caught in the air and banked in for the victory. Earlier in the season, I had hit a half-court shot at the end of the first half in a meaningless game at Wilkinsburg, but I had never made a shot of that magnitude. Perhaps one of cheerleaders in the group transposed the earlier shot into the Penn Hills game and had convinced the others of her inaccurate recollection.

I must admit that I had a fleeting impulse to correct their mistaken memory of that final game, but the words to Billy Joel's song flashed in my head, "Leave a tender moment alone." Why let the facts ruin their treasured memory. If they wanted to remember me as a hero, they had every right. Besides, it might embarrass them if I pointed out their mistake. Who knows, maybe Danny Krow will go back to his twentieth reunion, and the girls will remember his final shot landing gloriously dead center. He deserves some of my special karma.

Danny's team had an outstanding senior class. The angular Michael Orr exceeded all of my expectations and blossomed into a bona fide threat. Dawson Huff bounced back from being cut in his sophomore year to being a key player and a part time starter in his senior year. Bryan McKinney emerged as a tenacious clutch shooter, and Matt Leiderbach moved in from California, a free-styling Christian rapper who was refreshingly eccentric. Danny, of course, was their leader. His pride washed over the entire team. It was his squad, and everybody's play was elevated because Danny cared so much. It wasn't the phony "rah, rah" cliché bullcrap that teammates can see through. It was a pulsating hunger to chase perfection and never be satisfied with yesterday's performance. His pride arose from an intensity of vision that few players ever generate, and from a form of self-love instilled in him long before he walked onto my basketball floor.

BEDROOM BANNERS

PRIDE

Everything I've ever done was out of fear of being mediocre. *Chet Atkins*

Respect yourself and others will respect you. *Confucius*

An invincible determination can accomplish almost anything and in this lies the great distinction between great men and little men. *Thomas Fuller*

HUMILITY
Champions show gratitude.

"TODAY, I CONSIDER myself the luckiest man on the face of the earth." This iconic line was spoken on July 4, 1939 by Lou Gehrig of the New York Yankees who was dying of ALS (amyotrophic lateral sclerosis) a virulent disease that attacks the human nervous system. Earlier in the season, Lou voluntarily took himself out of the starting lineup for the first time in 2,130 straight games because he knew something was dramatically wrong with his body. Dubbed the IRON HORSE by the press for his amazing durability, Lou Gehrig addressed an overflow crowd at Yankee Stadium who had come to honor him one last time. There was no self-pity. There was no blame. There was only the humble recognition of blessings that he enjoyed in his brief thirty five years. Although this event took place decades before I was born, I get a lump in my throat every time I see the black and white footage of his farewell address. No one has ever displayed more grace, class, and humility than the great Lou Gehrig did on that day.

Humans typically are concerned with their own self-interest. It seems encoded into our DNA. We fight against our basic nature when we elect to allow a merging car into the tediously slow exit line in the stadium parking lot, or hand a few coins to a homeless veteran begging at a traffic light. Each generation, therefore, needs to be socialized to see the advantages of sharing and caring, as well as the perils of selfish behavior. True humility arises not so much from recognition of our personal flaws and fallibilities but from an acknowledgement of the rights, concerns, and uniqueness of others.

The code of the athlete was much different in the first half of the 20th century. Before the seismic shift in the 1960's, civility / humility was the rule. The great heavyweight champion Joe Louis was a gentleman both inside and outside the ring. Before a match, he would climb into the ring, walk over to his opponent to shake hands and wish him good luck. In press conferences the discourse was always respectful and full of praise for the opponent. Self-promotion, gloating, or boasting was taboo. In the 1960's Joe Namath and Muhammad Ali turned the sporting world upside down. Broadway Joe strutted down the streets of Manhattan in full length fur coats and made his famous "guarantee of victory" in Super Bowl III. Muhammad Ali (aka Cassius Clay) spouted poetry, predicted the rounds in which he would knock out his opponent, wore tassels on his boxing shoes, led cheers in between rounds and invented the flashy 'Ali Shuffle', the 'Ghetto Whopper' punch, and the 'Rope-a-Dope' defense. He "floated like a butterfly and stung like a bee" and announced at every occasion that he was the GREATEST OF ALL TIME. Though many of us recognized the originality, complexity, and generosity inside this stunningly talented athlete and showman, there is no doubt that he and his ilk opened Pandora's Box for the boorish imitators that followed. Many of today's greedy, pampered, over-indulged, me-first brat-letes have taken a misguided cue from the 60's generation.

Humility has a way of blindsiding some people. A few years ago Hall of Fame baseball player Willie Mays and his wife walked into a relatively empty multiplex theater at a San Francisco mall. The eight people in the theater started to applaud. Willie paused, waved, and then said, "It's nice to know that some people still remember." A guy in row four said, "I'm not sure who you are or what we're supposed to remember, but the management said there have to be at least ten paying customers or they won't show the movie."

I have my own 'slap in the face' humility story. I assigned an in-class persuasive essay on CELEBRITIES AS ROLE MODELS. About ten minutes into the class a girl raised her hand and sweetly said, "Coach King, can we use you?" With all the fake humility I could muster I said, "No, I don't think I'm really that big of a celebrity. I mean, I'm in the local papers and our games are on cable and stuff, and I occasionally get recognized, but there are lots of people more famous that you should write about." She looked puzzled for a second then said, "No, Coach King, I mean can we use the pronoun "you."

Nothing damages a team more than selfishness. The "disease of me" as Coach Pat Riley describes it corrodes the tenuous fabric of team unity. Players who obsess over statistics – how many shots they get, how many points they score, how many times their play is called –are potentially interfering with the only stat that matters – the score at the end of the game. I contend that the only three individual stats worth keeping in basketball are charges, floor burns and stitches. Everything else will take care of itself. If a team commits to those lofty standards of hustle, then selfishness disappears from the equation.

A few years ago, a team in our league produced a great player. Drew Kelly blossomed into perhaps the best big man Williamson County had ever seen. This man-child dominated virtually every game he played in from ninth grade until he graduated. In his senior year he set a single game scoring record of 67 points in the legendary KING OF THE BLUEGRASS TOURNAMENT in Lexington, KY. This Christmas tournament hosts teams from all over the country and his achievement had national implications. At the end of the regular season, all of the district coaches met to vote on all-league players and the MVP. Drew had either won or shared the award the previous two years. When nominations were opened, Brian Kelly, Drew's father and head coach spoke up, "This might seem a little strange, but Drew asked that his name not be placed on the ballot. He feels that he's been blessed with a number of accolades already this year, and he would like some of the other great players in the league to get the recognition they deserve." We all looked at each other in curious silence. We were genuinely moved by the maturity and humility displayed by this eighteen year old. Ordinary teenagers wouldn't dream of refusing another trophy or plaque to add to their treasure trove. Drew Kelly refused to be ordinary.

PERSONAL STORY OF INSPIRATION:

Two hours before game time, shortly after his team arrived for a crucial cross county showdown, opposing coach Darren Henrie bounced into my office and the first thing out of his mouth was, "Barclay for Nelson even up. No cash considerations or throw-in players. I give you Barclay, you give me Nelson." Though much younger, Darren and I had been friends for years. He had played at a rival high school in the 80's, then was an NAIA all-American at Lipscomb University where he played for the legendary Don Meyer. After graduating from college, he spent a couple of seasons working out with my team three or four times a week before shipping off to be a "hired gun" for some South American or Far East pro-team that needed an American sharpshooter.

I said, "Are you crazy? You'd give up Barclay (a 6'7" scoring machine who in his last four games had scored 34, 29, 27, and 24 points respectively) for my Anvil Nelson (an undersized post player with very average seasonal stats)?

He laughed and said, "No. I'm not crazy. Let's go, even up. What do ya say?"

Although the whole conversation was 'tongue-in-cheek' I pursued it further. "Why would you want to give him up?"

"Nelson's a warrior. You can depend on him to show-up every night. He's got heart. He hustles on every play, he's serious, he competes. I'd give up points to be able to coach character. My kid has no work ethic, he has zero leadership skills, he's a clown in the locker room, and basically he doesn't really care if we win or lose. I'd take a kid like Anvil any day."

"Well, you can't have him," I chuckled, "he's a franchise player with a no-trade clause."

I was surprised by Coach Henrie's insight into Anvil Nelson's character. I had no idea that Barclay was such a disappointment. The boy had haunted my dreams for the previous four days, trying to figure out a way to slow him down. He had incredible hands and a deadly touch. He was virtually unstoppable once he got the ball in the paint. Yeah, he seemed a little soft, but every player can't be a tiger. On the other hand, Coach Henrie spoke about Anvil like he had grown up with him in the same house. How could his assessment be so pinpoint accurate just scouting him in a game or two throughout the season. At the end of the night I checked the scorebook: Anvil Nelson had 17 points and 12 rebounds. Roger Barclay had 22 points and 4 rebounds. We won by nine points.

Anvil Nelson was a coach's dream – bright, eager, hungry, respectful, tireless, competitive, coachable, but most importantly, humble. Years earlier I was working a basketball camp with Mike Roller, one of the most successful high school coaches in America. He imparted some wisdom that I never forgot, "Every year coaches will have some terrific kids on their team, boys that will 'run through a wall' for you. So, isn't it only fair that we also have to coach a jerk or two as part of the deal?" I thought it over and quickly agreed; however, by having the opportunity to coach Anvil, I was going to finish my career way ahead on the balance sheet. This kind of young man comes around once every twenty years. He was one of the hardest working and most coachable players I have ever coached. He led the team with a quiet strength and was a fearless competitor, but more than anything his life was a model of the deepest humility.

During Christmas break of his senior year, Anvil sprained an ankle. He had to miss a few days of practice and watch from the sideline in a boot. As practice progressed I was getting more and more annoyed with the team's effort. We had a formidable opponent in a couple of days and the boys just seemed to be going through the motions. Despite the increasing agitation in my voice and some outright threats, the intensity level still wasn't there. After a series of suicide sprints and other assorted old-school fatigue inducing activities, it finally dawned on me why I was hating my team that day – Anvil was missing. Right then I interrupted practice and voiced my observation. I said, "Guys, I've just had a revelation. I think I've discovered the problem with today's practice. Anvil's on the sidelines. I had totally underestimated the energy, the hustle, the vocal encouragement that he gives you every night; and now when he's not out there all of you guys become 'ordinary.' Are you telling me he is that important to this team? Are you guys willing to go through this torture every night? Somebody better step up until he gets back."

At the end of practice when the boys were lined up on the baseline for the ritual foul shot closure, I looked over at Anvil and said, "See what you did to these guys today? You better hurry up and get that ankle healthy, man." He just glanced down and sheepishly grinned.

I'm pretty sure Anvil's senior year was fulfilling. He started every game, was a beast on the boards, averaged around thirteen points a game and received some post season honors. His junior year was a completely different story, however. Anvil's size, frame, athleticism and aggressive nature seemed more suited for the football field than the basketball court. He had played the sport in previous years, but for some reason he just didn't enjoy it. His first and only love was basketball, so he made a decision in the spring of his sophomore year to concentrate on basketball. It was extremely difficult for him to walk into Coach Crawford's office right before spring football and tell him his decision, but he had to follow his heart.

Five years earlier I had to make a similar soul searching decision. After being a head coach for thirty years, I walked into the principal's office and announced my resignation. Leaving the sport was like getting a divorce. It was a game that I deeply loved, but somehow you just know when it's over. Walking out of Hillsboro's gymnasium on a damp February night in 2003 after a region loss in the first round, it became clear. There had been inklings and hints for a few years. All of my own children were grown and no longer shared the bus rides and mid-week scouting trips. Even my youngest daughter Metta found a new world apart from the high school sports scene. The wins were less enjoyable and the losses more nagging and wrenching. The surge of renewal that I got each spring to plunge forward with next year's team was beginning to ebb. There are hundreds of coaching styles, but mine was more suited for a younger man. The intensity was becoming harder to muster, and I did not want to join that fraternity of coaches who choose to remain in coaching for the measly paycheck. It was time to pass the torch.

A bright young coach was hired from another school inside the county. Coach Randy Hatley and I became great friends, and he flattered me on many occasions with sincere requests for advice. Anvil was a freshman the year that Coach Hatley decided to give up coaching to pursue his doctorate. The job was mine again if I wanted it. After four years away from the sideline, I tortured myself for weeks trying to make the decision. I would be 57 when the season started. An entire cycle of players had passed through the program. I would be starting from ground zero, but the rising eleventh grade class was loaded, and there were a couple of gems in the rising tenth grade class like Anvil Nelson. With conflicted emotions, I climbed back into the coaching saddle.

It was in Anvil's junior year that I discovered the depth and source of his character. In high school sports there is something unexplainably unique about the junior year. First of all, boys have passed through puberty and most are at or near their full physical dimensions. Skill levels improve only incrementally at this point, and if a player has true varsity potential, he should be seeing some meaningful game minutes by this time (of course there are always exceptions and special circumstances). It is usually in a player's junior year that he first tastes the full rewards of varsity glory. He tends to romanticize the attention and bask in the fragile bubble of momentary importance. In his mind, each game is merely a prelude to future greatness. This is the last year that most players fantasize about getting a scholarship or playing major college basketball. By Christmas of their senior year the dream gets redirected as reality sets in. Anvil had an excellent summer season before entering his junior year. He played major minutes in the twenty five team-camp games. There was some inconsistency, some problems with losing the ball on crowded rebounds, some untimely passing decisions, but for the most part he provided quality contribution. The problem was, that we were returning six of our first seven players from the year before. In my mind Anvil would be challenging for a starting position when the league games started in January. In the games before Christmas, Anvil was in the rotation doing a credible job of backing up our 6'6"all-state center Kyle Teichmann. Unfortunately for Anvil, the bench got shorter and shorter as the season progressed later into the year. His playing time slowly decreased as the mistakes he made from inexperience became magnified as our drive for a league championship heated up. I found it necessary to keep the six seniors on the floor in some combination for the entire game.

Anvil simply needed more seasoning, so I now began dressing him for JV games. Ordinary boys would view this move as a gesture of disrespect and a demotion. They will pout in their body language both on the floor and on the bench. Their sour attitude becomes a drain on the team and on their coaches. Eventually, the parents will want a meeting to discuss their son's unfair treatment. I learned long ago, that this is an ordinary response to try to rescue not only their son from his embarrassment and disappointment but themselves as well.

These meetings are inevitable and they come with the territory. I courteously agree to meet with the parents just once. I will explain my decision calmly and respectfully. I try to make it clear that I have not lost faith in their son and that I am committed to his development as a player and as a person. On a couple of rare occasions, however, a parent's agenda was to inform me how blind I was to his son's talent and that everybody knows he should be a starter. I then force the parent to tell me which player he should start ahead of. When he gives me a specific name (John Doe) I give him this option, "You know, you might be right, but I wonder if John Doe's father would agree with you. I'll tell you what, if you can get Mr. Doe to come in here and tell me that your son should start over his son then I'll change my mind.

Anvil wasn't ordinary. Deep down I knew his lack of playing time *really bothered him. He had quit football, he had played an important role all summer, he was getting significant minutes early in the season, and now he was relegated to JV status. Instead of sulking and caving into the easy responses of rejection, he simply increased his effort.*

There wasn't a single let-down in practice, and he played every minute of the JV games like it was the seventh game of the NBA finals. During varsity games he would verbally encourage his teammates and greet them with high fives and fist bumps when they jogged off the floor for time outs. In the locker room after victories, there was never the selfish indifference while others were celebrating. He was the consummate teammate.

Anvil's actions that season became an essay on humility for me. By comparison, I remember my own experience with being benched in college for a spell, and the petty way I reacted toward the teammate who had taken my spot. I don't even belong on the same page where Anvil's name is written.

The bottom line is that humility is the conscious attempt to control the ego, that part of the psyche that can deceive us into inflated self-importance and foolish actions. What was the source of Anvil's humble strength? The answer is predictable but abundantly clear – his parents.

Being a teacher and a coach, I get a chance to peek inside some windows to get small glimpses of a player's home life. I met Anvil's mother at open house in his sophomore year. Anvil was a student in my 8th period honors English class. His mother, Deneice, was a tall no-nonsense woman who was very serious about her son's education. She was an elementary school teacher and requested a meeting the first night we met. She wanted to discuss the curriculum and Anvil's performance to date. The meeting lasted an hour, and it became clear that she had expectations not only for her son, but also for me in the class room. I was impressed and a little intimidated by her devotion to her son's academic life.

Mr. Nelson was a little different story. When I resumed my coaching career, the first activity of the summer was to load the team into the school van and head to The University of Tennessee at Knoxville for a team camp. The first parent who introduced himself to me in that back parking lot was Anvil Nelson, Sr. Big Anvil was a burly African-American whose George Foreman handshake engulfed my diminutive hand. I later learned that Anvil senior had been a Division I college wrestler at Illinois State although the years had rounded and padded over a once powerful frame. He thanked me for inviting his son to go to camp and for chaperoning the boys over the weekend. He patted his boy on the shoulder and said, "I'll see you Sunday, son." Young Anvil answered, "Yes, sir."

Ironically, on the first day of camp, young Anvil caught a nasty elbow to the scalp and needed several stitches to stop the bleeding. We spent several hours in the emergency room getting him patched up, and I overheard the conversation with his father when he called him on my cell phone. The tone of respect he used, and hearing him sign off with "I love you, too," impressed me. There weren't many fifteen year old males in my experience who displayed such trusting affection for their old man. The next day Big Anvil showed up in Knoxville. He looked over the wound and said, "How do you feel, son?"

"I'm fine."

Young Anvil had a sizeable chunk of hair shaved out of his head, and a big white patch of gauze covered the stitches like a cockeyed racing stripe. I still laugh to this day at Anvil's reaction when he looked into the mirror seconds after the doctor sheared him like a sheep. He kept blurting out the words, "Oh my God. Are you kidding me?" I guess even the most humble among us can still have a touch of vanity.

Two years later I got the chance to have a lengthy conversation with Big Anvil at another summer team camp. He had volunteered to help carpool the boys down to Birmingham Southern University and one evening we sat in the cafeteria and talked for a couple of hours. His life's journey and business achievements were intriguing, but he also revealed a stunningly powerful event that has echoed through the decades in the Nelson family. When Big Anvil was a senior in college, his father had been randomly murdered by two white men as he came out of a restaurant and was walking down the street. The event forced him to give up wrestling so he could devote more of his time to becoming the family patriarch. Other family tragedies soon followed, but if anyone was emotionally equipped to respond with strength and decisiveness in a crisis, it seemed to be the man across the table. Through the years during each parole hearing, Mr. Nelson made sure that he was physically present to ensure that the pain of the family was represented. This was the man who was helping to raise the remarkable young man I was coaching at the time.

In September of his senior year, Anvil stopped by my classroom after school. "Coach, can I ask you a favor. Ah, if you don't mind, could you look over my college essay and just tell me what you think. Make any corrections or if you have any suggestions, I'd appreciate any feedback." I told him I'd be glad to.

After he left I began to read one of the most moving tributes to a father that I have ever come across. He filled two pages with gratitude, love and honesty. Each line revealed touching examples of paternal love and sacrifice that helped to shape his son into a perfect model of humility. Here is an excerpt from the essay:

". . . I cannot begin to express the kind of impact he has made in my life, but I know that without his love and guidance, I would not be the person I am today. As I have grown, our relationship has evolved from a boy and an authority figure, to a young man who seeks wisdom from a respected and trusted mentor. He has inspired me in so many ways that as I get older, I just hope I'll be able to walk in his oversized shoes."

Mark Twain once said, "When I was fourteen I thought my father was the stupidest man on the face of the earth. When I turned twenty one, I couldn't believe how much he had learned in just seven years." The quote speaks to the adolescent stage of being embarrassed by our parents before we eventually appreciate their sacrifices and goodness. Anvil, it seemed, never succumbed to those feelings. He had it figured out long before the great Mark Twain ever did.

BEDROOM BANNERS

HUMILITY

The main ingredient of stardom is the rest of the team.
John Wooden

How far you go in life depends on your being tender with the young, compassionate with the aged, sympathetic with the striving, and tolerant of the weak and strong. Because some day in life you will have been all of these. *George Washington Carver*

This is the final test of a gentleman: his respect for those who can be of no possible value to him. *William Lyon Phelps*

You have reached the pinnacle of success as soon as you become uninterested in money, compliments, or publicity.
Thomas Wolfe

God wisely designed the human body so that we can neither pat our own backs nor kick ourselves too easily.
Author Unknown

You're never as good as everyone tells you when you win, and you're never as bad as they say when you lose. *Lou Holtz and John Heisler, The Fighting Spirit*

TRAIT **8**

CHARACTER
Champions make right choices.

AS A YOUNG coach I copied some questionable tactics that I learned from older coaches. When a foul was called during a scramble on the floor, I would immediately signal for our best foul shooter to step to the free throw line hoping that the referees didn't know who was actually fouled in the pile-up. I rationalized that it was the referee's job to get it right. In my mind, I was simply doing some clever coaching to get us a couple of points.

Another questionable coaching technique was teaching an offensive player to demand his space when he was being harassed by an opponent. If a swarming defender got too close, a quick pivot with elbows extended would clear the area that was rightfully his. If a sharp elbow made contact with some facial bones, it was simply collateral damage.

About ten years into my career, I decided that the above techniques were not really in the spirit of the game. Perhaps I came to this realization after I was on the receiving end of the strategies, but nevertheless, something in the pit of my stomach was telling me that these tactics were dishonorable. The player who was fouled should shoot the free throws, and nobody deserves to get a broken nose for guarding too closely. I just decided to stop coaching that way.

Bobby Knight was perhaps my most influential role model as a coach. He revolutionized the game of basketball. He is regarded as an uncompromising coach who ran his programs with unimpeachable integrity. In 1976 I attended a clinic in Washington D.C. specifically to hear him speak. It was about this time that women's basketball was starting to assert itself in colleges by demanding equality in budget and facilities. The teeth of Title IX were starting to be felt. Six hundred coaches assembled in a huge hotel ballroom, and Coach Knight had just taken the podium after the morning break. Two minutes into his lecture, the back doors opened and two female coaches walked in holding donuts and coffee cups. Knight looked up and saw them walking down the aisle toward the front row. After staring at them in silence for twenty seconds, he went ballistic.

"You god-d----d women want the same rights, the same pay, the same respect as men but you can't even get your lazy a - - - s in here on time. You want to munch on your donuts and stay out in the lobby gossiping when your butts should be sitting here taking notes and trying to soak up everything you can."

The two shocked women sunk into their seats mortified.

He went on in that same vein for another few minutes then calmed down and began to talk about his "100 Most Important Points of Basketball." When he started to address the topic of player motivation, he got a little smile on his face and turned to the two scolded women sitting up front and said, "Could I have the two of you women who walked in late come up to the front here for a little demonstration." The two of them came forward with some hesitation then Knight continued, "Here's what I want you to do, ladies. When I say go, just run over as fast as you can and touch the wall, then run back here as fast as you can. READY GO!"

Self-consciously, the two of them jogged to the wall about a hundred feet away, turned around, and ran back. All of the coaches applauded politely.

"Very good," he said. "Now, if you don't mind, after you catch your breath, I want you to do it once more, only this time I'm gonna add some motivation. READY GO!"

When they started to run, Knight began screaming maniacally into the microphone, "MOVE, RUN, LET'S GO, MOVE YOUR A- -." The two of them ran dramatically faster than they did the first time. All of us were laughing and enjoying the visual illustration of his method of motivation even though it was done at the expense of two naive women who dared to invade our male fraternity.

"See," he said, "that's motivation. Just by my raising my voice, they moved twice as fast. The same thing is true for your team. Players need to be motivated. They'll run faster, jump higher and play harder when someone gets on their a - -."

I still admire Bobby Knight, but through the years he seemed unable to sense the subtle shift in society that was slowly reinterpreting his colorful behavior as unacceptably boorish. The image of those women running to the wall has haunted me for over thirty years. I felt a twinge of embarrassment for them at the time, but I am even more embarrassed that I allowed myself to enjoy their discomfort. I lacked the character to suppress the feeling. It wasn't until my daughters were born that I realized the collective shame we should have felt in that ballroom. I can't imagine what my reaction would have been if one of my daughters was coerced to run to the wall for the amusement of six hundred ex-jocks.

The writer H. Jackson Brown said, "We build character piece by piece: by thought, choice, courage and determination." Every one of us must make hundreds of moral choices each day. Should I stop completely at a stop sign (no cops are around), do I recycle the water bottle (there's only a trash can in this room), do I share the gossip (nobody likes her anyway), do I ask for the questions on next period's quiz (I had too much to do last night), do I hold the door open for the next person coming behind me (they're walking too slowly), do I cut line to join my friends in the cafeteria (everybody does it), do I claim my extra bedroom as an office on my tax return (there is a computer in there), do I let my friends in free when I'm selling tickets at the movie theater (they would do the same for me). Character is always under construction. Having the confidence to do what is right even when it is inconvenient or unpopular requires uncommon inner strength.

An athlete shows character in hundreds of ways: rolling out of bed at 5:00 a.m. to run, or swim, or pump weights, pushing oneself in every drill no matter if a coach is watching or not, never stooping to dirty tactics to get an unfair advantage, never retaliating to trash talk, never cheating with performance enhancing drugs, and never uttering the following sentence, "I'm not making excuses, BUT . . ."

Benjamin Franklin revealed in his autobiography that as a young man he believed he could become morally perfect. He created a list of thirteen virtues that are, in order: Temperance, Silence, Order, Resolution, Frugality, Industry, Sincerity, Justice, Moderation, Cleanliness, Tranquility, Chastity, and Humility. He set about creating a weekly plan by which he would master one virtue per week eventually perfecting them all. Once he mastered the virtue he would move on to conquer the next one. He believed that he could become morally pure and be able to make the right moral choice in every situation. Although it was a noble experiment that deepened his self-understanding, young Ben eventually realized that perfection was unattainable. In the end he humbly rationalized that maybe it was good to have a flaw or two so that others would not be jealous.

Every year during our study of the play *JULIUS CAESAR*, I good naturedly search for one "honest" man just like Diogenes. When we come to the line, "For who so firm that cannot be seduced," I have some fun testing the value system of my students. With mock seriousness I fabricate the following scenario. "You guys aren't aware of this, but I use this teacher gig merely as a front for my other job – Drug Lord. Now, this weekend, I need one of you to make a run to Florida to pick up a huge shipment of heroine that just came in. All you have to do is leave early Saturday morning, park the car in the hotel parking lot, then get up on Sunday and drive back. The drugs will be in the trunk when you get up and you don't have to see or talk to anyone. I'll give you $5,000 before you leave and another $5,000 when you get back. Who wants to make the easiest $10,000 you'll ever make in your entire life?"

I then call on a random cross section of the class to see who is willing to accept the mission. If they refuse I simply increase the amount I am willing to pay until they agree to do it. I am always amazed at how many of them will eventually agree to betray their own moral values if the price is right. When the potential reward begins to outweigh the potential consequences, many people abandon their core values. How many scandals have ruined careers in politics, business or sports? The news abounds with tales of greed, lust and corruption that literally destroy lives, all resulting from a fundamental abandonment of character. The good news, however, is that invariably in every English class to date, I have found a student or two who refuses to be ordinary and claims they are incapable of being "seduced."

Perhaps the most moving depiction of character I have ever witnessed occurred in the tiny town of Parkersburg, Iowa in 2009. Ed Thomas, the revered head football coach of the Aplington-Parkersburg Falcons for the previous thirty-four years was murdered in the school's weight room by Mark Becker, a former player with a history of mental illness. The incident became national news and devastated the entire community who were still recovering from a deadly tornado that ravaged the town a year earlier. Coach Thomas was a coaching icon, a pillar of integrity, a molder of men, and a bastion of small town values whose life was defined by devotion to his faith, family, town, school, and team.

In a tragedy of this dimension the natural impulse of surviving family members would be to seek immediate revenge, to lash out in anger and demand swift retribution. Often times the extended family of the perpetrator is forced to suffer the shame and stigma of the crime through subtle shunning or complete ostracism. The ripples of a crime often touch the lives of innocent and good people. The Thomas family would not let this happen. In the early moments of their deepest grief they realized the pain that the Becker family was experiencing. The families attended church together. The older brothers of the shooter as well as the shooter himself had played for Coach Thomas. The Thomas's reached out in love to comfort and console. They made a public appeal to the community to be aware that two families were grieving and in need of healing and that the Becker's needed the town's love and support as well. This remarkable gesture of decency gave living testimony to everything Coach Ed Thomas had ever preached at home, in the locker room, and in the way he lived his life. His family's choices in the days after his death honored the memory and character of a great man.

PERSONAL STORY OF INSPIRATION:

The odd thing about coaching is that the boys are immortal. Through the years my black hair thinned and turned gray as I rounded into middle aged softness. The boys, however, were always sixteen and lean. Each era produced its own superficial trends – hair length, slang, the length of the uniform shorts; but a young boy's hunger always looked the same- eager eyes in quest of the holy dunk.

Relating to young athletes is a tricky art, especially when your own life drifts deeper into the sober land of adulthood. We think that we age at glacial increments, but in reality, the seasons zoom by. It seemed like one day I was playing one-on-one against my best player after practice, and the next day I was sending the manager to the drug store for laxatives.

Sports psychologists have many theories on why some coaches can stay in touch with younger generations while others become irrelevant as they age. Leadership is not about following a manual. It is more art than science. John Wooden did not win a national championship until he was 52 years old in 1964. I'll bet that at no time in his life could he have named the four Beatles, but that didn't matter, his effectiveness resulted not from being in touch with pop culture, but by being in touch with human nature. He was a great coach because his players intuitively sensed that he was fair, he was knowledgeable, and he meant what he said.

In my experience, getting a group of young men to overachieve on the basketball court boiled down to a few simple principles: 1.Be enthusiastic 2. Be totally prepared 3.Use the pronouns 'we', 'us', 'our' 4. Call the boys by their first names. I tried to practice these principles throughout my career.

One of the most interesting relationships I ever had was with a young man who graduated in 1976. A coach should never play favorites, but he cannot help having them. Stanley Sabin was introduced to me on a football field while I watched him run pass patterns during some informal summer workouts. My eyes were drawn to a little ninth grade fireplug with shoulder length hair. The kid was quick, ran crisp patterns, and caught everything he touched. I was intrigued by the combination of hair and talent so I asked an assistant coach what his name was.

"Oh, he's one of yours. That's Stan Sabin. His brother Sam is a junior. He's a tough little kid. I don't know if he'll ever play here. Hafta grow." Then he yelled out, "Hey, Stanley, STAN come over here. I want you to meet Coach King. He's the new basketball coach."

Stanley stretched out his hand, looked me dead in the eye, nodded, and said, "It's good to meetcha."

I joked with him and said, "It must be pretty hot under all that hair? Do you think it'll all fit under your helmet?"

He smiled cautiously, and said, "Maybe, maybe not, but I don't catch the football with my hair."

Oooh, the little man stopped me in my tracks. I liked him right away.

"What about next winter when you're dribbling up the court and someone steals the ball from you when you're brushing the hair out of your eyes?"

He said, "I'm like a sheep dog. They don't seem to have any problem with all that hair in their eyes."

He was quickly growing on me.

"Well if you're gonna play for me little man, you better have some pit bull and some Doberman bred in."

This was my introduction to Stanley. I sensed a piercing intensity tempered by a trip-wire wit. I soon learned that those same darting blue eyes that saw holes in an opponent's full court press, also saw holes in the logic of small town conformity that stifled the genius of this rural maverick. Years later Stanley confirmed the depth of character that I recognized in him very early in our relationship.

Basketball, like all sports, is a very simple game. At the first coaching clinic I ever attended, a famous college coach told everyone to always apply the KISS principle- Keep It Simple, Stupid. A lot of coaches feel compelled to clutter their philosophies with the newest trends. When UCLA had their great teams, everyone started using their 2-2-1 press. When Kentucky won a championship with big bruisers, everyone pounded the ball inside. When Arkansas smothered teams with their 40 Minutes of "HELL" everyone face-guarded and trapped. A coach must stay true to what he teaches best. He must resist the siren sound of fashion. He should make some adaptations according to talent, he should add some wrinkles to keep things fresh, but he should not commit to some seasonal philosophy that compromises his core beliefs. When a coach complicates a simple game, productivity decreases.

This principle of simplicity escaped little Stanley. Perhaps it plagues all people whose teeming intellects are boxed by predictable convention. Stanley had the most curious mind of any student or player that I ever coached. He needed to know, "Why." Why are we running our plays to the right side every time? Why should we play a zone on out of bounds under the opponent's goal? Why should we hold the ball for a last shot at the end of each quarter even though we're behind by five points? His inquiries were endless. His fertile mind needed answers. And he was starting to annoy me.

My training told me that players should be indoctrinated like soldiers. They should learn to blindly obey orders. In the heat of combat, a soldier's life is threatened if there is hesitation. During one practice early that season, Stanley stopped in the middle of a play, held the ball under his arm and asked, "Why does the wing cut over the top of the down pick? Shouldn't he cut under the guy on the block?"

I lost my temper, blew the whistle, told the whole team to get on the baseline, and I began screaming, "What makes you think I want to hear anybody's opinion on anything. From this point on, you will keep your mouths shut. I'll talk, you'll listen. You play, I'll coach. I'm the damn captain of this ship. The only time you open your mouth is to call a play, communicate on defense, or to encourage a teammate. If I catch you whispering, smiling, or laughing, I'll run you until at least five of you babies quit. You understand me?"

I blew the whistle again and made them run five suicides (full court staggered sprints) under 28 seconds.

It was classic "old school" fear tactics, but I followed through on my threats. For the rest of the year I ran that team like a sadistic French lieutenant in Napoleon's army. If a player's shirt tail was out, the whole team would run suicides. If I blew the whistle and a player was in the middle of a shot, he'd better scramble to get the rebound before it hit the floor, or the whole team ran suicides. During full court scrimmages, if I observed two players smiling on the sideline because of something one said under his breath, the whole team ran suicides. Our team wasn't very good, but we would have won the Suicide State Championship that year if they had one.

It wasn't until two years later when Stanley and I were riding together to watch an all-star game in Pittsburgh that he revealed a personal experience that made me question my discipline tactics.

He said, "You know Coach, one day right after a Saturday practice I was helping my Dad build a shed in the back yard. I was mixing cement for the footer; he was sawing some pine boards. Mom came to the back door and yelled out something to Dad. He stood up to answer her then turned around and bumped his forearm on the corner edge of 2 x 8. He hit it hard enough to draw a little blood. I heard him say, "Damn, I been gored by a board!"

Dad's a funny guy, but right when I started to chuckle, I caught myself and stiffened up with a serious look on my face so he wouldn't catch me laughing. I guess I didn't want to run suicides in the back yard."

His story made me realize the potential damage that indoctrination can have. My misguided desire to control the way my players thought and behaved carried over into their personal lives. All abuse of power springs from a dark well of insecurity. I must have felt profoundly inadequate in those early days, but those wonderfully resilient country boys hung in there with me and they left their guts on the floor every game night.

After that conversation with Stanley, I reevaluated some of my draconian methods. I needed to coach smarter, not tougher. It's a fine line between conditioning for punishment, and conditioning for victory.

Over the next two years Stan and I had hundreds of other conversations that included religion, social issues, politics, ethics and sports. He was blossoming into a first rate free-thinker, but there seemed to be a precocious restlessness in his questions. He was far from sullen, however. In fact, he relished cleverness and the witty banter of playful insult more than anyone. He would explode in laughter at an appropriately stinging retort. But in his senior year he was faced with making decisions about his future, and he was being tugged by conflict and self-doubt.

Some of this doubt was fueled by the climate of the times. In the middle 70's the country was still reeling from the deep divisions caused by the Vietnam War. Young Americans questioned authority at every level. The mantra of American youth was that "nobody over thirty could be trusted." The country was divided into hostile camps fueled by the hippie rhetoric of rebellion. Traditional "apple-pie" patriotism was dismissed by many young people as sentimental pandering to irrelevant traditions. Older people bristled with deep indignation when young people showed disrespect to the flag and other national symbols. Many college aged kids openly regarded the police as uniformed "pigs" and would taunt them when they were a safe distance away.

In my second year as the basketball coach at Slippery Rock High School, I was driving on Route 8 going to my parents' house following an evening practice. I still looked very much like a college student with fairly long hair and a tie-dyed T-shirt I used when I played pick up ball. A local radio station was going off the air and was playing the "The Star Spangled Banner" as it did every night at 8 o'clock. I cranked the volume up and for more than two miles I sang every word to our National Anthem at the top of my lungs failing to notice the policeman whose lights were flashing behind me trying to get me to pull over for speeding. When the song ended, I finally saw the lights and heard the siren.

A very agitated middle aged cop with a crew-cut walked up to my window and began screaming at me, "What's your problem boy? Don't you know you're supposed to immediately pull over when you see my lights?"

"I didn't see them, I swear, officer."

"Well, what were you doing that you didn't notice my flashing lights and siren," he barked.

"Well, officer," I said haltingly, "I was singing The Star Spangled Banner."

"Get your butt out of the car right now," he yelled. He proceeded to give me a field sobriety test then scoured my car for illegal drugs. When he couldn't find anything he finally wrote a citation for going four miles over the speed limit. When I signed the ticket he snapped it out of my hand and said, "You college long-hairs are ruining this country. You better keep your nose clean, punk."

The American military was even more maligned by the youth counterculture than the police were, and Stanley was being pressured to accept an appointment to the United States Military Academy at West Point. To many, he seemed like the perfect candidate. He was a bright, disciplined scholar with outstanding grades and terrific SAT scores. He had a rich athletic background in basketball and foot-ball. He grew up in a small rural town where they still had Fourth of July parades and ice cream socials. But most importantly, Stan Sabin was a born leader. His peers listened to him. He was articulate and persuasive.

His entire support group of caring adults from guidance counselors to parents pushed him to accept the appointment.

"You'll be representing your country. You'll be able to retire at the age of forty. You'll be getting a $100,000 education for free," were some of the words of advice that were given.

Stanley finally agreed and accepted the appointment.

Late in the fall of Stan's first year at West Point, the Army football team traveled to play the University of Pittsburgh. A number of cadets were permitted to travel together in an excursion to support the team. He was allowed a few free hours to visit his parents, so he swung by my apartment for a quick chat. Stan shared that everything was going well at school. His professors were demanding and inspiring, he was having a little bit of trouble in Russian, and that he was playing in the 150 pound intercollegiate football league. His hair was shorn, and he was impeccable in his dress grays. He showed me the operational orders that were given to all cadets who made the trip. They were formatted like a battle plan with the coordination of every troop movement down to the exact minute the cadets would exit the stadium. Even a Saturday afternoon football game was treated as an exercise in strategic war maneuvers.

The next time Stan visited me was late in the summer after his second year at the academy. He knocked on my door and walked into the room in civilian clothes. He sat down and said, "Well, I've decided to leave West Point."

I was stunned.

"What are you saying?"

*"I'm leaving the Academy. I've decided that I do not want to be an army officer. If I go back I will be obligated to be a soldier for a long time. I know in my heart that the service is not right for me. I'm starting to become somebody that I'm not sure I want to be. Have you ever read the book **The Great Santini?**"*

"No," I said.

"Well, when you do, you'll know exactly what I'm saying. See, Coach, if I don't leave now, I'll be committing my entire life to

something that would not be right for me and unfair to my country who is footing the bill for my education. Believe me, my experience at the Academy has been life-changing. My small-town eyes were opened to a world I never knew existed. I sat in classrooms and rubbed shoulders with some of the most brilliant minds of my generation. There is history and greatness everywhere you turn on that campus. On one level, I wish I had the single-minded zeal and love for the life of a soldier that "Bull Meecham" had in Conroy's book, but I don't, and you know I could never fake it.

"Was there a problem? Did something go wrong? What about your grades? Were they Okay?" I asked.

"Oh, yeah, A-minus overall. As a matter of fact, earlier this summer I finished number one in Ranger School down at Fort Benning. I was designated as the 'Distinguished Honor Graduate.' Believe me, Coach, that was a pretty big deal."

"Did they try to stop you from leaving?" I asked.

"Oh, my God! They put me through the ringer. I had interviews with the battalion commander, the regimental commander, and I was even escorted into the office of the Commandant of Cadets who's a brigadier general. They told me how much this country had invested in me. How short sighted my decision was. How I would be viewed as a quitter for the rest of my life. What a disappointment it would be to my parents. That I was taking the easy way out."

I looked Stanley in the eyes and said, "And you held your ground?"

"Yes, sir."

"Man!" was all I could say. I stood there staring at him. After a few seconds I asked, "Where do you go from here?"

"I'm not sure. I need some time off. I'll stay with my parents for a while. I'll figure something out. If you don't mind, I'd love to come up and work out with the team this summer."

"Absolutely," I said. "My soft little guards need to be dogged by an ex-army ranger. We'll see you Tuesday night."

He laughed and we shook hands.

Stanley walked out of my apartment into a cold uncertain world.

We lost touch after a few years, but I'll never forget his resolve to follow his heart. It would have been different if he had been washed out of the academy because of grades or temperament, but he had been a model cadet. It would have been so easy for him to rationalize, avoid confrontation, and take the path of least resistance, but he followed his conscience despite enormous institutional pressure. How many young men would have had the character to make the right choice. I still marvel at the inner strength and self-possession that Stanley displayed so many years ago as a tender nineteen-year-old. Through the years, when I have grappled with a gnawing personal decision, the image of Little Stanley standing in my living room materializes into focus like an old Polaroid snapshot. There he stands with those darting blue eyes explaining his life-changing decision with conviction and simple eloquence. To this day I salute his courage. When faced with a momentous crisis of choice he made his stand and didn't blink.

BEDROOM BANNERS

CHARACTER

What you <u>do</u> speaks so loudly, I can't hear what you're saying. *Ralph Waldo Emerson*

Character cannot be developed in ease and quiet. Only through experience of trial and suffering can the soul be strengthened, vision cleared, ambition inspired, and success achieved. *Helen Keller*

Mishaps are like knives that either serve us or cut us as we grasp them by the blade or the handle. *- James Russell Lowell*

Ninety-nine percent of the failures come from people who have the habit of making excuses. *- George Washington Carver*

Adversity causes some men to break; others to break records. *William A. Ward*

CONFIDENCE
Champions visualize victory.

A COMEDIAN ONCE said, "When I was kid I was terrible at sports, then I found out that you could actually buy trophies (pause). Now, I'm good at everything."

True confidence requires two things: 1. Small bricks of achievement placed on top of one another to create a sturdy foundation. 2. The habit of thought that continuously reinforces the single minded belief that one is deserving of success.

Every human being who ever lived has been plagued by bouts of self-doubt at some point in their lives. The greatest, the smartest, the richest and the most powerful have all questioned their self-worth at one time; however, they all share a secret that is available to everyone – CONFIDENCE IS A CHOICE. A champion refuses to allow temporary setbacks, failure, and rejection to define them. A champion recognizes then expels negativity as soon as it seeps into his mind. A champion will cling to the visualization of ultimate victory until it is achieved.

About thirty years ago, it became politically incorrect to do or say anything that might offend the sensibilities of any young athlete. Damaging a young person's psyche was tantamount to Nazi persecution. The word "self-esteem" became a national buzz word and youth sports were transformed into Marxist experiments in praise, playing time, and trophy redistribution for all our little comrades regardless of individual differences and talent. This detestable term "self-esteem" was lobbed into the world of youth sports like a canister of tear gas. Self-esteem should not be confused with self-confidence. Praising kids indiscriminately or creating artificial success deludes them into a temporary and flimsy sense of self-worth. Self-confidence, however, comes primarily from building on a series of meaningful accomplishments. When players are held to extraordinary standards of effort and achievement, they begin to respect not only themselves but everyone else who shares those values.

Confidence is hard to define but easy to spot. Everybody is drawn to confident, decisive people who possess a sense of comfort with themselves. You see it in their posture, you hear it in their voice, you feel it in their hand shake, you detect it in the way they look you in the eyes. Confidence is nourished by a myriad of factors some of which may go back to the womb. When a child is raised with clear boundaries and with consistent expectations and consequences, he or she feels nurtured and safe. When parents, teachers, and coaches provide timely and appropriate recognition for true achievement, it gets deposited in a memory bank collecting compound interest daily. Hollow praise is as worthless as Confederate money.

I will not dispute that some children come into the world more genetically equipped to be confident. History is replete with unlikely success stories of people who overcame poverty and home dysfunction to prosper and achieve great distinction. Two presidents come to mind – Abraham Lincoln and Barack Obama. But confidence is usually an acquired trait built on the steady accumulation of personal successes. I often run into former students who were quiet wall flowers in the classroom ten or twenty years earlier then blossomed into thriving confident adults with beautiful families and successful careers.

As mentioned earlier, sometimes confidence is achieved by a conscious manipulation of attitude. I remember a story that my eighth grade English teacher Miss Overby told our class. When she was in college she and her best friend took a speech class together. The night before they were both scheduled to present their first speech, her friend went out on a date and did absolutely no preparation. Miss Overby wrote, revised, and practiced for hours fearing the moment when she had to get up and deliver. She remembered being so nervous when she got up to speak in front of her classmates that the speech fell flat and she received a 'C' minus. Ten minutes later when it was her friend's turn to speak, she bounced out of her seat in the back of the room, marched confidently to the front of the small auditorium and placed the notes she had just written firmly on the podium. She then glanced around the room, gave the entire class a friendly smile, and began to speak with clarity, volume, expression, gestures and eye contact. The speech didn't have much depth or substance, but she still received an 'A' minus. Miss Overby's friend had simply drawn from her memory bank of success, consciously relaxed, and performed with a sense of confidence and "swag".

Some of the greatest upsets in sports history have also resulted from simple attitude adaptations. The underdog decides or is coerced by a coach to simply dismiss the crippling emotions of self-doubt and fear and replace them with glorious images of victory. Closing one's eyes and visualizing the successful execution of game speed skills is often as effective as actual real-time practice. The mind does not distinguish between real or imagined successes. Both are recorded as dress rehearsals and stored to bolster confidence. Some coaches will have their teams practice cutting down the nets, hoisting trophies above their heads, or standing with arms raised in order to plant the power of possibility in their imaginations. These kinds of exercises energize players. Nerves, fear, and doubt do nothing but drain positive energy.

Coach Herb Brooks gave one of the most powerful pre-game speeches ever to his 1980 US Olympic hockey team moments before his collection of wide-eyed college boys shocked the world by beating the most feared professional hockey team on the planet. The Russians were expected to demolish the American amateurs, but once in a while a coach's words can alter destiny.

"Great moments... are born from great opportunity. And that's what you have here, tonight, boys. That's what you've earned here tonight. One game. If we played 'em ten times, they might win nine. But not this game. Not tonight. Tonight, we skate with them. Tonight, we stay with them. And we shut them down because we CAN! Tonight, WE are the greatest hockey team in the world. You were born to be hockey players. Every one of you. And you were meant to be here tonight. This is your time. Their time is done. It's over. I'm sick and tired of hearing about what a great hockey team the Soviets have. Screw 'em. This is your time. Now go out there and take it."

The rest is now history. The game is considered by many to be the greatest American victory of the 20th century. It is no secret that all Olympic athletes possess an uncommon level of confidence, but as humans I'm sure these future Gold Medalists had moments where their faith weakened, doubts crept in and dire imaginings of global embarrassment materialized like billowing black storm clouds. Coach Brooks created vivid scenarios that redirected his team's vision. Suddenly in their minds they were "skating with the Russians," and "staying with them" stride for stride, shot for shot. Suddenly, a vision of the passing of the torch, a changing of the guard was going to take place. There would be a new world order, and youth would be served. The crown would be snatched away, and their destiny fulfilled. The King is dead, long live the (new) King!

Herb Brooks was a great leader. Great leaders inspire. Great leaders have an unshakeable vision that they communicate to those who follow them. Great leaders are confident people who know where they are going and can help others get there with them. In his book **HOW GOOD DO YOU WANT TO BE,** Alabama head football Coach Nick Saban revealed that as a young coach, he thought that ranting and raving about a dropped pass was good coaching. As he gained more confidence through experience, it became clear that his job was to first and foremost teach the player the proper technique so that the mistake would not be repeated. He learned very early that coaching through intimidation was unproductive. In Coach Saban's words – "Fear kills passion."

Confident leadership by a team captain(s) is also imperative for success. Unlike most teams, I do not allow a vote to determine captains. Leaders simply emerge. Players will only listen to guys they respect, and the true team captain may not be the "rah rah" senior who thinks he is entitled to the position. In my experience a team captain demands that teammates practice with spirit, hustle, and purpose. He is a model of maturity, consistency, preparation, and confidence. His work ethic is contagious, his competitive fire spontaneously combusts throughout the team. That's the guy who will represent the team. That's the guy who will speak to the referees. That's the guy who will be an extension of the coach both on the floor and in the locker room.

PERSONAL STORY OF INSPIRATION:

"MVP my ass!" A.J. Krow's words jarred me a bit, but I glanced over at him and chuckled. We had just beaten Franklin High School in the 2009 District Championship game, our third victory over them that year. Our whole team was giddy after the overtime victory while the award ceremony was taking place at mid-court. When Franklin's star player Michael Young was announced as an All-Tournament selection, A.J. made his candid observation. A week earlier, Michael had been selected as a co-MVP of the league which apparently didn't sit well with A.J. This comment was a bit uncharacteristic for a straight "A", mature, student body president and team captain, but it captured a fundamental quality of self-assurance the likes of which I had rarely seen before in a student athlete.

Athletically, A.J. Krow was dramatically average. At 5'9 ½" and 155 pounds, he did not have great speed, strength or reflexes. As a point guard he had limited court vision, a weak left hand and he ranked as one of Brentwood High's most pathetic outside shooters of all time. As the starting quarterback on the football team, his passing skills ascended to mediocrity on his good nights and were embarrassingly negligible on most other nights. Yet, he led both teams to unexpected heights during his senior year through an uncommon understanding of winning intangibles, coupled with an irrepressible confidence in his ability to lead his teammates to victory. This kid was the poster child for refusing to be ordinary.

In A.J.'s junior year the football team started out 0-3. Before the season started, the coaches were convinced that a gifted athletic sophomore was the quarterback of the future and turned the team over to him. The results were disastrous. Four days before playing the cross-town rival who were state champions two years earlier, and state runners-up the previous year, A.J. was shifted from his position as a starting defensive back to the starting quarterback even though he had not taken a snap all year. Assistant coach Dan Winfree mentioned to me during the week that the team seemed to be inspired by the move. He said, "There's just a different feel in practice this week. I don't know how we're gonna play, but the guys have a different demeanor out there. A.J. just brings a steadiness and a confidence that we need at this point."

On the night of the game, A.J. executed the perfect ball-control game plan mixing an effective ground attack with perfect decisions on the option where he kept the ball on several crucial third downs. Down by the score of 7-6 late in the game, A.J. surprised everyone by unloading an uncharacteristically long heave to the left sideline for the 6'5" Chase Lyle who juggled the ball before falling into the end zone for the winning score. Brentwood had found its quarterback. The team went on a four game winning streak and were eventually eliminated in the state quarterfinals.

The following year A.J. blossomed into a great field general; however, about four games into the season, he got dinged up and had to sit out a game. He pleaded with the offensive coordinator to let him play. "Coach, I need to be in the huddle. Let me be a receiver. I might not be able to throw the ball but I can catch one. Or just be a decoy, but at least I could still call the plays." A.J. was convinced that being on the field, though hobbled, was better for the team than having no A.J. at all.

His football acumen was stunning. As a ninth grader he was contributing articles about the NFL draft to high profile websites. His insights and criticisms of NFL players and franchises were remarkably sophisticated. His father worried about some of the blistering feedback he was getting in chat rooms, and he nearly made him stop writing, but the passion was too strong.

*I told my assistant coaches on many occasions that we needed to check A.J.'s birth certificate. He talked and acted like he was twenty-five years old. He was articulate and well-read and so unflappable that it was unnerving at times. At the end of his junior season we were getting ready to play a regional game against a state Goliath. We were the fourth best team in our league pitted against the number two ranked team in the state of TN. We were supposed to be a slab of red meat thrown into the lion's cage. At the end of practice the night before the game, I gathered the team into a huddle to share some insights from an inspiring book. I said, "Guys, I just finished reading a book called **THE SECRET.**"*

A.J. spoke up and said, "Oh, yeah, I read that last year."

"Really? I said skeptically. "What's it about?"

"Well, it's about the law of attraction. Basically that you become what you think about the most, and that you attract into your life what you think about the most. The author believes that you can achieve your dreams by tapping into some cosmic power if you concentrate and focus on the results." I must say I was impressed by this junior in high school stealing my English teacher thunder, but apparently our little discussion had some benefits for the team. The next evening with two minutes left in the game, we were down four points. We ended up losing by seven, but Antioch's next three playoff wins were by an average of 45 points.

Sometimes, A.J. was simply audacious. In 2008 I had turned over all defensive responsibilities to assistant coach John Boucher. He began to implement a complicated match-up zone with some intricate rules and assignments. One day in practice while Coach Boucher was teaching it, A.J. strolled over to me on the sideline and said, "Hey,

Coach, we need to scrap this defense. It's not gonna work. We're never gonna get it. Let's just work on our "man to man" and perfect that. "

I said, "Be patient, man. Coach Boucher really believes in it, and I've seen some teams have a lot of success with it."

About five minutes later Coach Boucher sent the players for a water break and walked over to me with a big smile and said, "I think they're really starting to get it." I shook my head in agreement and decided it was best to keep A.J.'s observations to myself.

One time in A.J.'s junior year he had an absolutely terrible practice. He was throwing the ball away, just going through the motions on defense and not concentrating on anything. It was such an aberration that I turned to Coach Matt Bonds, a former standout point guard himself, and said, "What the hell is wrong with Krow tonight? We have a huge game tomorrow and he's completely out of it." It turned out that the school's annual LIP SYNCH contest (students dress up and mime hit songs while jumping around the stage in lame choreography) was being held in the auditorium that night. A.J. and some of his boys were performing the song YOUR BODY by Pretty Ricky in a few hours. When I found out the next day I was livid. I couldn't believe that our starting point guard would allow a distraction like this to detract from the focus needed to win a big a game. To me it was a form of betrayal, and we lost the game the following night. Instead of confrontation, I decided to let it slide. Coaches need to pick their battles. This seemed like a one-time event and perhaps I was overreaching for an excuse to explain the loss.

Fast forward one year to the exact same week. One of the reasons that I came out of a four year retirement was to have the opportunity to stop the incredible run that Franklin High was having in our district. They had not lost a regular season league game in three years, and in my first year back they whipped us three more times. The following summer I ordered maroon practice gear so that every day we would be reminded of the team that had dominated everyone over the last four years. I told the boys that when we end their streak this year, we would have a ceremonial burning of the jerseys and replace them with Brentwood blue.

We ended their four and a half year streak of 55 straight wins on January 16th 2009 on their floor. A.J. played brilliantly. Late in the game, in a play that has come to be known as "THE PASS," his man left to trap the ball. A.J. instinctively cut into the key to receive a return pass. An alert off-side defender tried to take a charge before he could put the ball on the floor, but A.J avoided him by whipping the ball around his back to Blake Eshenroder for a layup. Our crowd erupted and the incredulous buzz from the stands lasted for a good minute. I had never seen him throw a behind the back pass before or since. None of his former coaches can remember him throwing a behind the back pass. But in a packed gym in a momentous game, he had the instincts and confidence to flip it for a huge assist.

The next week after a tough road win, I decided it was time to organize the "jersey burning ceremony." Coach Boucher offered to host the team at his house on Thursday where we could burn the jerseys in his backyard out by the woods. To generate some anticipation for the ceremony I initiated a rare post-game pep talk and began to wax poetic. I got on a roll about the metaphorical significance of burning the jerseys; how it signifies the end of an era, that the smoke signals will tell the rest of the league there's a new kid on the block positioning themselves for a championship run. I went on about the fire that burns in our bellies and that these ceremonies were performed by primitive warriors since the dawn of time – blah, blah, blah. About this time Coach Boucher interrupted me and said, "Hey, Coach, I think A.J. wants to say something."

I said, "Yeah, A.J. what do you want to add?" I thought he might share an anecdote from something he read about Comanche or Mongol warfare to help heighten the effect of my speech.

"Ah, Coach, I don't want to spoil the vibe, but this Thursday is the Lip-Synch contest, and there are several of us that are involved in it. So I don't think we'll be able to do the burning ceremony."

My jaw dropped. I stared at him for five seconds and could feel *the blood rush to my face. "VIBE? VIBE? Is that what I'm doing up here, creating a freaking vibe?" I scanned the rest of the team and screamed, "How many of you guys are planning to be in that stupid show? Raise your hands." About six hands slowly rose. As a younger coach I would have drawn a line in the sand and snuffed out the distraction. If any of the players would have defied me, they would have been history as a member of the team; however, through the years I had mellowed and saw things through a little different filter. I said, "Alright, let me tell you sissies something. It's pretty clear where your priorities are. If you guys think that silly crap is more important than our mission then by all means go put on your little costumes and make-up Thursday night, but I'm going to tell you something so listen real carefully. The coaching staff will continue to work our butts off. We will continue to scout, plan, teach, strengthen and condition those players who share our goals. It's a stinking shame when old men want to win more than the players themselves. We have a chance to have a great year, but some of you guys would rather jump around on stage like a bunch of clowns and pretend to be rap stars. Maybe in March you can jump around in the bleachers watching two other teams compete in the Sectionals, and you can PRETEND to be champions." I smashed my clipboard against the wall and stormed out.*

I was 58 years old at the time of that tirade. It was probably a generational overreaction. I guess A.J. was really seventeen after all. The Lip Synch obviously meant a lot to him (and of course his group won the contest). His legitimacy as a winner was undeniable. My old school values generally served me well in most cases, but a modern coach might have embraced the Lip Synch, maybe have shown up and sat in the first row, applauded, laughed and then talked about it at the next practice. It could have served as a great team building exercise; however, I'm more like Rocky's boxing trainer Mick. I believe that eating raw eggs and soaking a boxer's face in salt brine is the only path to victory.

I had known A.J. since he was nine years old. He attended our summer basketball fundamental camps and even then it was easy to spot his positive aura of confidence. I would occasionally perform some simple magic and card tricks to entertain the group. A.J. would sit in the front row and always express his animated theories on how I pulled off the trick. Coach Boucher was his AAU coach for several of his middle school years, and would call me from various tournament sites to tell me what a shut-down defender A.J. was. "He's like a pit-bull. He WANTS to guard their best player. He begged me today to let him guard this kid from Alabama. And you should have seen him stalling in four corners. They couldn't get the ball from him."

A.J.'s crowning moment came in his senior year in the District Championship game. Late in the fourth quarter Franklin had an eleven point lead. Earlier in the game they had surprised us by switching from their traditional man-to-man defense to a spread 1-3-1 zone and it was killing us. They decided not to guard A.J. since he rarely took an outside shot, and besides when he did shoot from the outside he drew more iron than a medieval blacksmith. By playing the zone, they could then concentrate on guarding our outside shooters like David Hood and Sam Orr. On three straight trips down the court, A.J. swung the ball from side to side, paused, then launched a 22' set shot from the three point range. All three shots arc'd toward the lights then splashed through the nets like a coin in a wishing well. The lead was cut to two points and our momentum could not be stopped. The only people more surprised than the Franklin coaching staff was the Brentwood coaching staff. Each time he whipped the ball through the nets, he jogged back on defense like he was Kobe Bryant.

I'm positive that A.J. knew this night was coming. Making three straight three-pointers is not a noteworthy achievement in itself, but given the time, score and importance of the game his clutch perfor-mance is magnified. It sprang from a rare sense of self possession. He had performed on so many big athletic stages growing up that he sim-ply channeled past successes and seized the moment. He had no fear of failure. His self-assurance and belief in himself had been reinforced by a thousand visualizations of success. He now had one more vivid snapshot to put into his mental victory album.

BEDROOM BANNERS

CONFIDENCE

I've missed more than 9,000 shots in my career. I've lost almost 300 games. 26 times I've been trusted to take the game winning shot and missed. I've failed over and over and over again in my life and that is why I succeed.   *Michael Jordan*

No one can make you feel inferior without your consent. *Eleanor Roosevelt*

You gain strength, courage, and confidence by every experience in which you really stop to look fear in the face. You must do the thing which you think you cannot do.   *Eleanor Roosevelt*

Pay no attention to what the critics say. A statue has never been erected in honor of a critic.   *~Jean Sibelius*

It's not who you are that holds you back, it's who you think you're not.   *~Author Unknown*

Whether you think you can or think you can't - you are right. *~Henry Ford*

Nothing great has ever been achieved except by those who dared to believe that something inside of them was superior to circumstances.   *~Bruce Barton*

We probably wouldn't worry about what people think of us if we could know how seldom they do.   *~Olin Miller*

COURAGE
Champions conquer fear.

I REMEMBER THE words of the late Eddie Futch, who was in Joe Frazier's corner during the "Thrilla in Manila." The fight was one of boxing's most sensational bouts. It was a titanic struggle etched forever in boxing lore. In the fourteenth round Ali dished out incredible punishment, and Eddie decided to stop the fight before the final round. Joe strenuously objected on his stool. He still had a chance to win a decision, but Eddie Futch knew that Joe's courage could literally get him killed. The words of comfort and appeasement that he uttered to Joe Frazier in that corner are now famous. He leaned into Joe's ear and said, "Nobody's gonna forget what you did here tonight, Joe."

Courage is the most highly regarded human virtue. Every culture admires it above all others. History books regale us with countless stories of people whose physical, moral and spiritual courage catapulted them from the ranks of the ordinary. War heroes such as Alvin York or Pat Tillman, moral heroes such as Susan B. Anthony or Martin Luther King, spiritual leaders such as Mother Theresa and Gandhi are distinguished by one common and singular trait - their remarkable courage. Their entire lives were guided by a commitment to principle, and each one had to face hostility and haters who tried to sabotage their work. We all can admire public courage on this level, but courage comes to most of us in quiet whispers when no reporters are around to publicize our private triumph over fear. We have opportunities to display courage in countless actions throughout our lives, and often these obscure little victories will inspire those around us.

A few years ago I cut a player who tried out at the end of his freshman year for our summer roster. Each spring I hold tryouts for summer ball. The tryouts are basically a formality. When all of the returning players are finished with their spring sports, we hold tryouts designed primarily to help us choose a few rising sophomores to go to summer team camp. Although this player had been an occasional starter on our ninth grade team and possessed some decent basketball instincts, he was a tad slow, physically undeveloped and an erratic shooter who upon occasion displayed a hot hand. More significantly, however, I believed that he had questionable character. I had been forewarned that he had already had some scrapes with the law for various juvenile infractions. Coaches aren't social workers, so I decided to pass on this kid whose reputation preceded him. That summer we went to four team camps, played about twenty seven games and had next year's depth chart pretty well figured out. In the fall, the young man showed up at our organization meeting for strength and conditioning. He sat in the back of the room and filled out all the information. Over the next two months he attended every workout both in the weight room and on the track. I decided to cut him again in November. I still had my doubts about his extracurricular behavior, and I overheard some unfortunate teacher comments about his attitude and behavior that confirmed my decision. We had a great season that year and I was excited to get started up again for summer ball. That spring James had disappeared completely from my radar. For most kids, getting cut once is a clear message, but getting cut twice can be unmistakable. The coach does not have any plans to keep him on the squad. On the evening of spring tryouts the following year, I went to the school an hour early to sweep the floor and get the balls out. When I entered the gym, James was alone on the dimly lit floor shooting at the other

REFUSE TO BE ORDINARY

end on a side basket getting warmed up for his third tryout in a year and a half. He refused to look up at me, but just kept shooting and retrieving. I said to myself, "Are you kidding me? Man, this kid's got guts. How many times is he going to 'put himself out there' only to have his dreams crushed." I must say that the courage to make himself vulnerable a third time truly impressed me. Yes, he brought some baggage, but I decided that I was going to take a long, hard look at the kid because anybody who wants to be part of a team this badly and is willing to risk a third humiliation must have some substance to him. During the first lay-up drill he loped in then bounced toward the rim with a grace and explosion that I hadn't seen in him before. He had obviously been working extremely hard on his skills. Another factor that didn't hurt his prospects was his growth spurt of about four inches since his first tryout. Over the next two days, James was a model of hustle and heart. He defended with tenacity, dove for loose balls, rebounded with aggressiveness and banged in shot after shot. His perseverance paid off. Against some seriously slim odds, James earned a spot on the summer roster and had a terrific summer season. He was by far the most coachable kid on the team and immersed himself in our culture of discipline and hard work. By Christmas he was a starting guard on the varsity. Very few players were as devoted to personal improvement as James. He squeezed in more off-season court time in his two years as a varsity player than most do in a lifetime. His zeal for the game was refreshing, and basketball became a wholesome outlet for all of his misguided energy. In his senior year he led the team in scoring, was MVP of the district tournament, and was voted onto the all-region team. James Cox refused to be ordinary. His quiet courage changed failure and rejection into personal triumph.

One of the intriguing aspects of sports is that it provides a window into the psychological makeup of each competitor. Every day players are placed in positions of contrived stress, and their reactions are studied with meticulous attention. The team itself is a de facto family, and the same dynamics that play out in the home are often mirrored in the locker room, huddle or team bus. An astute coach can provide a stunningly accurate profile of every player who ever played for him. Thousands of dollars could be saved on Rorschach Inkblots and Myers-Briggs personality profiles with a quick phone call to the client's football or basketball coach.

One of the highest compliment clichés that a player can receive from a coach is the acknowledgement that " he would be willing to run through a brick wall" for the team. Although the metaphor is a simplistic exaggeration, this is courage in its rawest most primitive form. When a player is willing to risk personal injury for the achievement of a goal, his level of commitment cannot be challenged. The receiver who runs a slant across the middle risks decapitation. The soccer players who jump to head a corner kick risk mutual concussions. The baseball catcher who protects the plate on a throw from center field risks a violent collision from a determined opponent sprinting at full speed. This is a time honored mentality that harkens back to the Spartan motto, "Come back with your shield or on it!"

Courage is all around us and courage is in every one of us. Courage takes many forms and is the noblest of all human pursuits. From the humblest apology to the most daring military success, the history of civilization is a quilt of human courage. We must recognize it, encourage it, and practice it.

My uncle was stricken with Lou Gehrig's disease when he was 52 years old. Red Cavanaugh was tall, handsome, and proud. He was married and devoted to my mother's sister Peg. He drove the coolest cars, dressed with impeccable taste, sang old Irish songs with perfect Celtic pitch and was adored by his two children and all the nieces and nephews of the extended family. He was told by his doctors that he had three months to a year to live. The news was devastating, and my Aunt Peg prepared for a year dedicated to caring for the man she loved. The progress of the disease began as predicted. He noticed a degeneration in muscle control of his extremities. At first his foot would drag and catch on the rug causing a slight stumble. His ability to write or set his watch slowly disappeared. His speech began to slur, and eventually he was confined to a wheelchair. I remember, however, that every time we visited him, he was always cheerful, positive and never once displayed a trace of self- pity. I often saw him wheel himself over to the kitchen sink, pull himself to a standing position and begin to wash the dishes in a noble attempt to remain useful for as long as he could. Eventually, when he lost the power to speak, you could still see his eyes twinkle in appreciation of a good joke or funny story. It was painful to see a man who was once so vibrant become helpless and dependent. Surprisingly, and perhaps miraculously, Uncle Red lasted through the year. In fact he survived the next year and the year after that. To the amazement of every doctor who treated him, he survived for nearly thirteen years with my Aunt Peg constantly and lovingly at his side.

The courage to remain positive in the throes of a debilitating terminal disease is rare and revealing. Thousands of people each day must brave the horrible indignity of illness and live with the awareness that they are dying. But also remarkable is the courage of the caretakers whose sacrifices too often go unnoticed. Aunt Peg had to feed, clothe, bathe and move my uncle from his bed to the wheelchair and back again each day. She had to maneuver him into the car for doctor visits. She sat patiently with him each night watching TV, reading to him and doing everything to make him as comfortable as possible. I once asked her in private if she felt any resentment for her life being so restricted by the demands of the disease. She said, "Oh, heaven's no! I am so blessed that the Lord let him stay with me for as long as he did. I'm not saying that it was easy, but each day Red was alive I counted as a gift." Uncle Red died peacefully in his chair in October, 1985 with his courageous and beloved Peg right there beside him.

STORY OF INSPIRATION

During the Civil War, Union troops sometimes reported a strange phenomenon when encountering the Rebels. Upon occasion Southern boys would ignore all safety and ride screaming into the jaws of certain death. Their blood curdling "Rebel Yell" haunted the Yankees' dreams.

Had John Boucher been born a hundred and sixty years earlier, he would have marched with Nathan Bedford Forest and the Army of Tennessee. At the battle of Shiloh when his regiment was ambushed and surrounded, he would have galloped screaming across an open field straight into the smoke and booming cannon fire. In this final death ride, wielding a rifle with bayonet attached, he would take out one last bluecoat devil before he fell in a death gurgle on the soil of his beloved South.

In the 1980's, however, this soldier charged into a different kind of battle with the same suicidal fervor every time he stepped on the floor. Ironically, he played basketball for a transplanted Yankee coach in Brentwood, Tennessee.

John was one of the least physically imposing players I ever coached, but no athlete ever did more with less. He was 6'1" with newspaper stuffed in his sneakers. He had rounded shoulders atop a pear angled body, a weak chin, blue eyes, a crew-cut and bad hands. On the third day of school in my second year at Brentwood High, I was called to the office over the loudspeaker. Standing by the counter was a large broad-shouldered Viking woman who dwarfed her timid looking son. The receptionist said, "Coach King, this is Mrs. Boucher. She wants to talk to you about basketball." I shook her hand and she introduced me to her son, John, who shook my hand a bit too eagerly, his wide eyes begging to make a good first impression. Mrs. Boucher spoke again with commanding authority, "We're transferring in from Brentwood Academy. I'm not happy with the basketball program over there. I think he'll get a fairer shake over here. His Dad is 6'4" and was a starter on Hillsboro's best teams in the 1960's. I was the leading scorer on the women's team. He's gonna grow. Now, I know he'll be ineligible this year, but we're making the move anyhow. How do we get him into your eighth period basketball class?"

This woman was strong. Her eyes were angry rapids that splinter male egos on sharp rocks. John, in the meantime, was staring at me and nodding his head in agreement with every word his mother voiced.

I said, "Well, I'll see what I can do. You'll have to talk to his guidance counselor. That's who'll make up his ---." She interrupted, "Where's his office?"

That was my first meeting with John Boucher and his mother "Big Mama Bouch" which she would soon be called by the entire Brentwood basketball family and several of the referees, administrators and fans around the county.

The first time I saw John play was a few days later. Many schools in the South build practice time into their academic schedules. Coming from Pennsylvania, I was astounded that a public school would even consider the use of academic time for basketball training. Teams in Tennessee could practice literally all year round, and to this day, many schools still permit it. To me, it took the "extra" out of extracurricular. No one believes more in dedicated hard work than I do, but my paradigm for personal improvement incorporated a time to let the fields lie fallow, to separate players from coach, so that they return in the summer with fresh ears and legs. Players should have the freedom to play pick-up ball on outdoor courts or at rec centers for a few months where they can experiment on moves and shots without the judgmental eye of their coach.

In one ten-minute pick-up game, I realized that John Boucher was a terrible player. I wasn't even sure if he was worth keeping. He was slow, couldn't dribble, was too short to play inside, and couldn't shoot well enough to play guard. In those eighth period pick-up games, however, I did notice how much he frustrated and annoyed the older players with his "Bonzai" style of defense. He made "bulls in china shops" look balletic. Every time his man picked up a dribble, John would bounce against his chest and scream "DEAD, DEAD, DEAD" and wave his arms like a psychotic windmill. Whenever a loose ball popped free, he would dive headfirst skidding across the floor like he was saving a baby falling out of a tree. His knees and elbows were scabbed and re-scabbed in pus-lined strawberries. He blocked out on every shot, chinned every rebound, sprinted back on defense to stop all easy scores, and he took charge after charge on every pretty penetrator that invaded his turf around the goal. Of course, in the code of pick-up games taking a charge is taboo. This did not deter him. Penetrators would get up limping from their unexpected tumble then curse John the whole way down the floor. In his mind, he had a right to his spot on the floor, and he would not concede one single, solitary centimeter of precious paint.

How could a coach not keep a basketball "zealot" like John on the roster? Even if he never played one second of varsity basketball, this kid would make our team better just by turning him loose in practice. Besides, I was afraid his mother might kick my butt if I cut him.

In John's first season there was an incident in practice that set the tone for his career. In a particularly heated half court scrimmage, John was playing repeat defense against the first team as they were running the man to man offense. He was typically aggressive and inadvertently hacking everyone who came near him. When clumsy kids get tired, the foul ratio increases dramatically. From a set play, Glen Toney curled to the basket off a screen, caught a pass and fluidly turned to lay the ball in. John saw the play develop but got there too late and slashed Glen on the arm to cause him to fall off balance to the floor. Toney bounced up, trudged toward John then punched him square on the side of his jaw in blatant retaliation. I heard John grunt. He spun awkwardly from the force of the blow but kept his feet and didn't fall. Two players grabbed Glen and a third grabbed John who was clawing to break free. I immediately sent Glen to the locker room.

After practice, I called Glen into my office to discuss the problem. He said, "Coach, I just couldn't take it anymore. He grabs, fouls and hacks everybody on every play. He's plain dirty, Coach. Nobody can stand playing with him out there. He's a horrible player. He gets in everybody's way, he's gonna get somebody hurt, and he has that goofy shaved head. He comes in here from Brentwood Academy like he's all tough or something. I'm sorry that I hit him, but I couldn't help it, he deserved it."

I said, "First of all, son, you better learn to help it, because if it happens again, you're history around here. You understand me? I don't care how you feel about him. Nobody on this team slugs a teammate, EVER! Secondly, if you can't handle what Boucher's giving you, what are you going to do in real games when bigger, nastier guys than Boucher turn the heat up on you? You gonna punch everyone that gets under your skin? Because I want to tell you, if your best blind-side punch can't knock a sophomore off his feet, then you better be a hell of a good lover, because you don't have much of a future as a fighter." He glared at me for a few seconds with a healthy defiance then I told him to go get dressed. He reluctantly muttered, "Yes, sir." There wasn't another problem all year.

That punch tipped me off to John's unbelievable pain threshold. By the time he graduated, John took more charges than any other player in American high school history. There is no way to prove this statement since no official statistics are kept even on a state level, but night after night, John would plant his short-necked body in sacrificial stance inviting a collision that pounded him to the floor. When the referee would place his hand on the back of his head and point down court, John would jump to his feet and sprint down court in a kind of hybrid waddle-gallop.

Some purists would disagree, but the charge is the best play in basketball. It often takes away two hard-earned points, it places an additional team foul against the opponent, it can put a key individual on the bench with foul trouble, it can derail an opponent's rally, and it definitely injects adrenaline into your own team. It is one of the few plays in sports where courage can nullify talent. John developed the act of taking a charge into performance art. Long before reality TV, Boucher would orchestrate human collisions on the basketball court every night. When a lightening slick superstar stutter-stepped and knifed past his stiff kneed defender bounding toward the rim to crush a dunk, John Boucher would stand between the railroad ties and invite the train wreck. Often, I had to wince and turn away at the carnage of two tangled bodies on the floor. When I would look up again, John would be waddle-galloping down the floor.

In retaliation, opponents used to clobber John on the other end of the court. At a little over six feet tall, John was often guarded by larger, stronger players. In a testimony to Darwin's theory of adaptation, he developed a wide range of nifty moves that usually involved a series of pivots, pump fakes and step-throughs that ended with an uncanny and deadly accurate baby hook shot. His defenders became so frustrated that an undersized, untalented player who couldn't beat their team's mascot in a foot race was schooling them on the low post that they would eventually just club him to the floor when he faked them into the air. John would simply get up, dust himself off, march to the foul line and plop two shots cleanly through the net. In his senior year he was the most unlikely first team all-county player who ever played in the South.

One night John became involved in a very ugly post game scene when we were playing a Nashville city school. John played his typically physical game, but when he walked outside through the lobby doors to get on the team bus, two players from the opposing team attacked him, knocked him to the ground then stomped and kicked him before some of our parents swung folding chairs at the boys to finally chase them off.

John had taken a real beating. His mother took him to the hospital for x-rays. His ribs were severely bruised, and he couldn't play the next game. The two players who attacked him were only given a two game suspension by the state athletic association. A week later we taped a pad around John's ribs for protection. He played somewhat cautiously that night and only collected three charges for the game.

Because that incident was so potentially dangerous, I decided to do something that no other high school coach may have ever done. I knew that John had a way of annoying opponents with his style of play. I also believed there was another factor contributing in some way to the negative attention he got from opponents and referees – his haircut. Today, athletes all over the country shave their heads like

Michael Jordan or wear short burr cuts, but in 1986 when John was a senior, 98% of all high school students wore their hair considerably longer. John's cropped head made him look like a cross between Bart Simpson and Sluggo from the "Nancy" comic strip. He became an object of derision around the league, and it was my theory that his stubbled haircut made him a more visible target of fans, players, and referees. I had to make a coaching decision. I called him into my office right before Christmas and said to him, "John, I'm ordering you to grow your hair. I don't want you to get a haircut until the season is over in two months." He stared at me incredulously trying to figure out if I was serious, then he said, "But Coach, I like to wear my hair short."

"I know," I said, "But I think it's hurting the team. I think it's working against you."

At one time in the militaristic world of competitive sports, long hair violated the code of manliness. The World War II vets who returned to teach and coach, equated long hair with feminine weakness, or with California liberal fruitiness. Real men had crew cuts and marine buzzes. It eliminated the distraction of grooming and contributed to the uniformity of the troops. Real men didn't primp and blow dry. But the boomers changed the rules on just about everything including fashion, politics, education, art, media, sexual mores and the hair length of athletes.

John respected my request and let his hair grow. Two days after we were eliminated from the playoffs in 1987, he stuck his shiny buzzed head inside my classroom door on the way to first period and grinned like the Cheshire Cat.

After the post season banquet that year, John's father stopped me on the way to my car. He said, "Coach King, I just want to tell you something. When John was little, I coached his Junior Pro teams and I knew in my heart that he would never be a basketball player. He was just awful. I felt sorry for him because he tried so hard, but he just couldn't play a lick. Never in my wildest dreams did I think that he would be a starter on a large high school varsity team. I just want to thank you for having faith in him and sticking with him these past three years. He's had a wonderful experience in your program, and he exceeded every expectation I ever had."

"Thank you, Mr. Boucher," I replied, "but you realize it wasn't me that gave him that work ethic, and I didn't put that oversized heart in his chest. Somebody molded that kid long before I got a hold of him. I know it's a cliché, but basketball doesn't build character, it reveals it. Your boy had the biggest heart of any boy I've ever coached."

♪♪♪♪

Once players graduate, there is a transition period of a year or two before they stop aching for the bonds of brotherhood they experienced as players. Their withdrawal from the sport can be lengthy and painful. In some cases a boy will never experience again that sacred intensity of purpose. Nothing he will ever do will give him more meaning or identity than he had on those winter evenings when the world gathered inside toasty gyms to celebrate the rituals of his youth. Life will encroach, and nothing will ever quite approach the giddy urgency that is felt inside the huddle of a final time out.

John went on to play a couple years of Division III basketball, but unlike most alumni, he never lost contact with me or the boys in the Brentwood basketball program. When he was home from college in the summer, he would scour the inner city for the best street talent then bring them to the gym to scrimmage the boys. He would often coach my team during summer leagues and at team camps when I wasn't available or when I wanted to watch the team from a detached vantage point. After John got his business degree, he went back to school to get his degree in physical therapy. I hired him as an official assistant coach during this time. For six years I trusted him with the development of our post players, and he was an invaluable liaison between an aging coach and the younger generation of Allen Iverson worshippers. It was an interesting transition for John to go from a "whipping boy," sophomore grunt to a respected peer whose opinion I learned to value implicitly. In the early years of his assistantship, I treated him like a player, especially in the heat of a close game. John understood my volatile intensity, and dismissed it as "me" being "me," but his new wife had a huge problem with it. On numerous occasions he joked about her instructions to "tell me off." John would chuckle, "Yeah, Coach, she wants me to tell you that if you don't start treating me with respect that I'm going to quit." After a couple of seasons together, however, John evolved into one of the most astute assistants that I ever worked with. He walked into practice every single night ready to coach his "butt off." He was fearless in his suggestions, and his bulldog player personality rubbed off on all of our teams. We won well over a hundred games in his first six-year stint as my top assistant before being selected as the girls' head coach at the new high school opening across town.

The deciding factor in my return to the sidelines after a four year hiatus was that John Boucher agreed to be my assistant once more. By this time he was coaching a woefully talent-challenged girls' team at another county high school six miles down the road. In the late spring of 2007, we held our first organizational meeting to introduce ourselves to the players. John seemed totally on board, but he had not revealed his plans to his own team yet. His team meeting was scheduled at Centennial High School an hour after our meeting was over. I was unprepared for the phone call later that night. John was emotionally distraught. The meeting did not go well. He was not prepared for the tears, shock, and looks of betrayal that he got that afternoon. He said, "Coach, I feel awful. It's like I'm deserting these girls. They've worked so hard for me and I am just miserable. It's like every coach they've ever had has walked out on them, and now I'm doing it. I'm still coming to Brentwood, but I really don't know if I'm doing the right thing."

I listened for a while and realized that John couldn't live with his decision. "Look," I said. "You've got to follow your heart and do what your gut tells you. You're their coach, and they need you. I'm not sure that John Wooden could turn that program around, but if you want to beat your head against the wall down there for another year, this same job will be waiting for you next year. Luckily for me, he returned to BHS the following year.

No player ever was more supportive or cared more about sustaining the excellence of his high school program than John Boucher. He still bleeds blue and gold. He had a hand in shaping every single team that has come through the school, either by coaching them on the practice floor, banging with them in the hot summer gyms, or wearing #40 as a proud player. The courage and loyalty he showed this Yankee general was legendary. Nathan Bedford Forrest would have loved him. If the South would have had a few more boys like John Boucher, there would be a Confederate States of America just south of the Mason Dixon line today.

BEDROOM BANNERS

COURAGE

One man with courage makes a majority. ~Andrew Jackson

Courage can't see around corners, but goes around them anyway. ~Mignon McLaughlin, The Neurotic's Notebook, 1960

Courage is what it takes to stand up and speak; courage is also what it takes to sit down and listen. ~Winston Churchill

Courage doesn't always roar. Sometimes courage is the little voice at the end of the day that says I'll try again tomorrow. ~Mary Anne Radmacher

A brave arm makes a short sword long. ~Author Unknown

A hero is no braver than an ordinary man, but he is braver five minutes longer. ~Ralph Waldo Emerson

OVERTIME

I HAVE A singular vision of what I will do when I win the Powerball lottery jackpot. I'm going to charter a Caribbean cruise ship for one week and invite every boy who ever played for me on an all-expense paid luxury cruise during the week of July 25th (my birthday). In addition, they can bring their entire family - wife, kids, parents, in-laws, girlfriends, and their favorite teacher from high school or college.

I will also invite anyone who was involved with the basketball program over the past forty years - every manager, assistant coach, school administrator, teaching colleague, statistician, cheerleader, scorekeeper, PA announcer and bus driver as well as all of my high school and college teammates (I may even invite a referee or two). I will pay for all plane tickets, meals, lodging and of course every perk aboard the ship.

Aside from all of the usual entertainment, I will set up a week long basketball tournament that will include showdowns between a mix of different era players. I will be perched somewhere near mid-court with a bull-horn hurling light-hearted critiques of their diminished abilities. There will be free throw and three point shooting contests and an obstacle course time trial. On the last night, we will have the mother of all basketball banquets hosted by Dick Vitale, and we will give out all of the awards for the week's contests. We will also watch a professionally made video of game footage, highlighted by the hit songs of each era, narrated by Charles Barkley.

What a glorious week it will be - touching base with the remarkable young men whose lives intertwined with mine for a few brief seasons and catching a final glimpse of them as men. I will schedule time to meet with every one of them to learn of their wide and varied journeys that branched far from the sweaty gyms and heated huddles of their high school glory days. I can imagine the wonderful stories they all will be able to tell. I wonder whose dreams came true, what dreams they are still chasing, whose dreams got deferred? We will laugh and reminisce and argue and eat and laugh and drink and laugh some more.

Sometimes the filter of nostalgia sugarcoats reality, but I am grateful to every single player that I ever coached. What other profession encourages or permits an adult to peek inside the sacred window of a young man's soul to glimpse the potential and ennobling qualities that continue to fire human progress. Sometimes I naively think that if the Islamic extremists could meet the American boys and girls that I coached and taught, their fanatic pursuit of our destruction would cease. Contrary to their warped perception of Western society as evil, greedy and decadent, they would realize that America spawns goodness and tolerance and generosity. They would have to acknowledge that our people are ingrained with a core of the highest values that all great religions teach and cherish. Their irrational hatred would certainly soften once they got to know my boys.

♪♪♪♪

To this day I still shoot at imaginary baskets. Before I get up from the couch, I flick a perfect release toward a nonexistent hoop above the door frame. Walking down an empty hall at school, I'll sky-hook my keys against the wall and catch the ricochet in my left hand. Occasionally in my kitchen, I'll rock back and forth with an imaginary ball in a left handed dribble, then shoot a fade away a la Earl Monroe. The muscle memory of 50,000 jump shots runs deep in me and bubbles to the surface with regularity.

A grizzled old coach once told me after a game, "When I was young I used to get upset after a loss. Now, I just go home and sleep like a baby. Losing doesn't bother me a whit." I stared at him in disbelief then vowed to never become so pathetic.

I still marvel, however, at those guys in their late sixties and seventies who continue to coach with love and passion. During spring football practice last year, I drove past the practice field and slowed down to watch a few drills. Front and center was a seventy-two year old coach named Tom Crawford with his baseball cap spun backwards on his bald head barking out instructions, jogging with the boys from station to station and demonstrating technique with animated gestures. I shook my head in wonder. Coaching still revved him up.

Throughout my career, one of my favorite things to do late at night especially in October was to shoot by myself in the high school gym, lit only by the neon exit signs and the light that seeped in from the hallways. We all need our quiet sanctuaries. Some people have their fishing holes or park benches or little cafes where they go to escape and recharge their batteries. My sanctuary was a faintly lit empty gymnasium. It became a holy place for reflection and creativity. The beauty of the game unfolded magically before me - the leathery feel of a ball spinning in my fingertips, the trajectory of a shot in flight, the fluid balance of a continuity offense meshing perfectly in front of me in ghostly formations. My giddy faith in the boys and our potential to have a great year would bubble over in those darkly quiet moments interrupted only by the sound of a swishing net-click or the echo of a stray ball bouncing away on the wooden floor.

It will be this sacred solitude that I will eventually miss the most. Life only has meaning in reflection. It was in these quiet moments that I first realized the profound privilege that graced my life. Coaching young men for forty years in such an intense and intimate way opened portals to a higher understanding of myself. These eager boys who refused to be ordinary were tender metaphors for the highest ideals and lessons of life and defined for me the true meaning of a champion. I will always treasure what I learned from my boys while teaching them the simple game of basketball.

CPSIA information can be obtained at www.ICGtesting.com
Printed in the USA
LVOW102343090613

337708LV00005B/24/P